Business Credit Made Easy

The Secrets of Business Credit Revealed

Brian K Howard

Publishing First Edition

Brian Keith Howard

First Edition

Copyright 2015 by Brian K Howard

All rights reserved.

No part of this book may be reproduced in any form without written consent of the publisher, excepting brief quotes used in reviews.

First Printing 2015

Printed in the United States of America

ISBN-13: 978-1508602576

Introduction

It is estimated that over 90% of the business population knows nothing about business credit. As a result, many business owners use their personal credit for business purposes at great consequence. Over 50% of businesses today fail. With most of those businesses, the business owners used their personal guarantee for their business debt – costing them their family's entire life savings and personal assets.

With this book in your hands, you will become a business credit master. You will know exactly how to build your business credit score and create your business credit profile. The business credit profile you will build will help you obtain large amounts of credit and funding for your business without a personal guarantee and without you being personally liable for your business debts.

I have helped clients improve their personal credit, build business credit and qualify for financing. I have witnessed loans get underwritten and seen first-hand how lenders make their lending decisions. I have helped clients build and repair their personal credit to qualify for lending. Moreover, I have helped business owners obtain a substantial amount of dollars in funding.

I committed to learning everything about how creditors and lenders do business, which helped me create one of the most advanced business credit building systems in existence today. This system has helped business owners obtain funding and build business credit for their businesses. This system's unique business credit building methods are taught at well-attended credit conventions in the nation.

Your business can have an excellent credit score, and qualify for credit and funding without you having to offer a personal guarantee. This book will show you how.

This book will give you the knowledge and power to fight and win the business credit battle. It is designed to help you understand step by step the process of building credit and obtaining funding for your business. First, you will learn what the business credit system is. Then, you will be enlightened on what lenders are looking for when deciding whether to approve a business for credit and funding or not. Finally, you will learn where to go to secure funding for your business and know the types of funding available today.

Contents

Chapter 1	What Exactly Is Business Credit?
Chapter 2	Three (3) Major Business Credit Reporting Agencies
Chapter 3	Business Credit Scoring
Chapter 4	How to Build a Strong Business Foundation
Chapter 5	Business Credit Reports Made Easy
Chapter 6	Building Vendor Credit Made Easy
Chapter 7	Building Revolving Credit Made Easy
Chapter 8	Know Your Bank Ratings
Chapter 9	How to Get Business Funding
Chapter 10	Business Credit and Funding Is Available
Chapter 11	Personal Credit Matters

1 Chapter One

What Exactly Is Business Credit?

You have most probably heard of Equifax, Experian, TransUnion and the FICO score before. In the United States, these have become household names. On the other hand, most Americans, and even most business owners, have never heard of DUNS number, PAYDEX score, Intelliscore or Dun & Bradstreet (D&B).

Entrepreneur.com reported that fewer than 10% of business owners have any knowledge of business credit. This is actually great news for you. Now that you are reading this book, you are not only going to know about it. You will thoroughly understand the power of business credit. This means that since the other 90% of business owners know nothing about business credit, there is more money available for the smaller percentage – which now includes you – who do know about it.

Most business owners quickly get accustomed to using their personal credit as personal guarantee for their businesses. As a result, most never realize that it is possible to obtain considerable credit for their business with no personal guarantee or personal credit inquiry – hence, with no personal risk.

Business credit approvals are based on the credit profile and score of the business, not its owner. The business owner's personal credit profile is not reviewed at all. The business is approved for credit, not the owner. Meaning that in many cases there is no personal guarantee required.

Personal Guarantee

Most business owners currently use credit with a Personal Guarantee (PG). A personal guarantee is an agreement that makes the business owner personally liable for the business's debts and/or obligations. In case of a default, a creditor can pursue the business owner's personal home, bank accounts and investments, and file judgments against personal assets of the business owners. No PG means the business takes on the risk, not the business owner. This keeps their personal finances safe and secure.

One of the most common mistakes entrepreneurs make is using personal credit to finance their businesses. A recent study shows that 87% of ALL businesses mix personal and business credits. Common examples include paying for business expenses with personal credit cards and obtaining personal loans to finance business expenses. Business owners who do this may later on suffer from one or more of the severe and adverse effects in their personal lives.

When an owner personally guarantees business related financing, the lender will require a personal credit check. Every time an inquiry appears on an individual's credit history, his or her personal credit score is lowered. The lower the score the harder it is to secure financing and the higher interest is charged.

A further adverse effect on the business owners using their personal credit for business debts is that the more personal credit is used to guarantee a business, the higher the business owner's debt-to-income ratio will be. This means that the next time they apply for a loan lenders will only approve it if they apply for a lesser amount of money. This obviously impacts on the individual's personal life. Signing that loan for the business could prevent the business owner from getting a mortgage or a personal car loan.

When a business owner uses their personal resources or credit to finance a business, they chain their financial security to their company's success. If the company fails, the business owner is then left holding the bag, and their personal finances will be ruined along with their business. This reality is very possible, considering that over 50% of businesses now fail in the first 3 years, largely due to a lack of access to capital.

Each time personal assets are pledged for any type of credit extended to a business, the business owner jeopardizes their personal assets, including savings and investment accounts, cars and even their homes. If the business cannot pay off its debt, the bank will come looking for them *personally* to make good on the loan. It does not matter if the owner owns 25% or 100% of the business; the lender can pursue the person who supplied the personal guarantee for the entire business debt.

A business entity established as a sole proprietorship is most susceptible to this risk. Although the owner can build business credit as a sole proprietor, they will be completely liable for all personal and corporate debt.

Their credit history will be based solely on activity associated with their social security number because they do not have a corporate tax ID number. As a sole proprietor, they also have no legal means for separating corporate from personal credit.

Incorporate Your Business

The best way to protect personal assets is to incorporate the business. Having done so, business owners can then shield themselves from personal liability for the company's debts and will normally reduce their tax burden. Many business owners are unaware of the value of incorporation, and fewer understand the essential steps necessary for building the kind of corporate credit that will enable them to take full advantage of their entrepreneurial status.

Incorporation makes the business a separate entity with its own liability from the business owner. Incorporation separates business assets from the business owner's personal assets. If someone decides to sue the company, they cannot touch the business owner's house, car or anything else they or their family owns.

By incorporating the business, the business is also enabled to begin establishing corporate credit that will eventually provide the funds needed to grow the business and help it get to the point where it can obtain funding without a personal guarantee.

Financial Mistakes

1. Not building business credit

Many business owners are making big financial mistakes when it comes to business credit. One of the big mistakes is not building their business credit; they do not spend extra time and effort to build business and financial credibility for their business.

2. **Not paying bills on time**

    Another major financial mistake business owners make is not paying their bills on time. In many cases, this lowers the business credit score, making it harder to get new credit at good terms.

3. **Mixing personal and business credit**

    Another serious issue is the business owner mixing personal and business credit by using personal credit to pay for business debts. Investing personal credit and cash into the business is a big financial mistake. This may earn them trade credits, but those credits are not helpful in building business credit since they are not reported to the business credit reporting agencies.

4. **Putting personal assets at risk to business debts**

    Using personal credit cards, cash, line of credit, etc. to pay business expenses creates a big financial issue as it puts the business owner's family assets at risk to business debts. When this happens, the business owner is creating personal liability by pledging personal assets rather than utilizing corporate credit.

Most business owners do not manage their business credit, as they should, as an Asset rather than a Liability. A lot of business owners do not realize that business credit is an asset that grows with the business. A personal credit has a predetermined limit and borrowing ceiling, limiting what the business owner can be approved for. Building a strong business credit profile will help the business cash flow by reducing or improving vendor and supplier terms, credit card rates, financing costs and insurance premiums.

To know if building business credit makes sense for them, a business owner should try to answer the following questions:

- Have I ever **been declined** for a business loan or financing?
- Could I use a business **line of credit** for working capital?
- Do I need, now or in the near future, to **lease equipment?**
- Am I currently stuck having to **personally guarantee** every loan?
- Would I like to obtain easy, fast approval on credit cards for my business?
- Do I currently receive the most favorable credit terms from vendors?

There is an unfortunate lack of useful information available on how to finance a business, especially when it comes to building business credit that will allow a business owner to finance, operate and expand the business without putting their personal finances or their family's future in jeopardy.

When a business owner applies for credit for a business, most creditors will pull the business credit report. This credit might have been used for anything in the business from credit cards, to equipment and auto loans.

Build a Strong Business Credit Rating

When a lender pulls a business credit report, and there is nothing there, they will rely on the business owner's personal credit to guarantee the financing. If there is no business credit file, they are not able to lend as much credit to the business as they would if the business has an established business credit file. A business credit report enables a business to receive more funding. Thus, it makes sense to build business credit. By building a business credit, business owners can save money for their business and for their family.

Building a strong business credit rating is vitally important to business success. Without it, the business owner will pay much more (higher interest rates) for the money they borrow – if they can get approved at all. In fact, banks, which say they want to help small business owners, actually turn down over 97% of all business loan applications. They do not make it easy for a business to get approved.

Let us look at a quick example. Supposing a business without a strong business credit rating needs $50,000 for a necessary piece of equipment, their bank will only use the business owner's personal credit as a reference. If they get approved, they will get (in this example) an interest rate of 18%. With a Dun & Bradstreet report, that business can have a lower interest rate – as low as 10% – without the business owner having to guarantee the loan with their personal assets. Look at the summary below.

	Personal Loan	Business Loan
Lease Amount	$50,000	$50,000
Interest Rate	18%	10%
Term of Lease	60 months	60 months
Monthly Payment	$1,269.67	$1,062.35
Total Payments	$76,180.20	$63,741.00
Total Savings		*$12,439.20*

By simply building business credit and setting up a business properly, the business owner can literally save tens of thousands of dollars. Business owners must pay close attention to this kind of savings.

It does not matter how long a business has been in business. As far as the banks are concerned, if that business does not have a business credit rating, they are only going to lend a personal loan with personal guarantees from the business owner. This creates multiple issues, as the average personal credit report gets just one inquiry per year and has 11 credit obligations, typically broken down as seven credit cards and four installment loans.

Business owners are not your average consumer because they carry both personal and business credit. This typically doubles the number of inquiries made to their personal credit profile and the number of credit obligations they carry at any given time, all of which negatively impact their personal credit score.

In addition, because business inquiries and personal inquiries are not separated on their personal credit report, their scores are negatively affected, too. At the same time, by using their personal credit history to get business credit, they are not able to build their business score, which could help them attain critical business credit in the future. The key to establishing a business credit profile and score is to find companies that will establish credit for your business.

Business Credit Basics

Business credit gives entrepreneurs a unique opportunity to build, maintain and acquire credit for their business and personal needs. That means business owners can build and grow their companies without having to rely solely on their personal credit.

In the United States, personal credit reporting agencies create a credit profile when a consumer with a social security number accepts their first job or applies for their first credit card. This profile gets updated whenever there is a credit inquiry, a new employment, an address change, a new credit account, or a public record data update. Eventually, the credit report becomes a statement of an individual's ability to pay back a debt.

In many cases, the same is true for businesses. When a business issues another business credit, it is referred to as trade credit. Trade or business credit is the single largest source of lending in the world.

Business credit bureaus gather information about trade credit transactions to create a business credit report using the business name, address and federal tax identification number (FIN), also known as an employer identification number (EIN), issued by the Internal Revenue Service.

The business credit bureaus use this compiled data to generate a report about the company's business credit transactions. Often, those issuing credit will rely on the business credit report to determine whether to grant credit to the business. If so, how much and at what terms should the credit be?

To qualify for most business credit sources, the business must have established a positive credit score with the appropriate business credit reporting agencies such as Dun & Bradstreet (D&B), Experian and Equifax. Once a positive business credit score is established, many merchants will then approve the business owner for credit in the business's name.

Thousands of major merchants offer business credit. However, most do not promote their business credit programs. They, therefore, are difficult to locate. Some merchants offering business credit include Chevron, Dell, Staples, Lowes, Visa, MasterCard and large banks like Wells Fargo and Bank of America.

Once business credit is established and paid as agreed, the business credit score will increase. As more positive credit history is established and credit score is increased, business owners can be approved for more credit with higher credit limits. With business credit established, the business can qualify for loans, credit lines, auto financing and mortgages.

Business credit is an outstanding resource for businesses. Owners can obtain credit to run and expand their businesses without the personal liability of using a personal guarantee.

Currently, information provided to the business credit bureaus is sent in voluntarily. No business is required to send it in. Therefore, in the case of most businesses, the credit bureaus never receive all or any information. Many companies go years growing their business credit without any of it being reported to the credit bureaus. Because of the lack of reporting and promotion of business credit by the credit industry, many entrepreneurs are not at all familiar with business credit. Due to this unfamiliarity, many business credit myths have been formed.

Business Credit Myths

A business has many of the same attributes as an individual person. Businesses earn income, file tax returns, pay debtors, use credit for the business and have credit histories.

Still, some business owners overlook the importance of a healthy business credit profile and score, or do not know anything about business credit at all. Because of this, many business owners believe the myths surrounding business credit instead of the real facts.

Myth 1: Merchants do not offer business credit.

Most merchants and major retailers offer business credit. They just do not advertise it. There is no upside for the merchant to promote credit with no personal liability if the business owner is willing to take on that liability. Therefore, they do not promote their business credit cards and regularly ask for an SSN.

For instance, Home Depot offers a commercial credit account but, in almost all cases, credit applicants are willing to provide their social security number and give their personal guarantee for the debt. Therefore, it does not make sense for Home Depot to offer the applicant a card with no personal liability if the applicant is willing to sign and give that guarantee, and accept the liability.

Business credit with no personal credit check or guarantee is available through Lowes, Home Depot, Office Max, Staples, BP, Shell, Wal-Mart, Sam's Club, Costco, Radio Shack and thousands of other major merchants.

Myth 2: Business credit limits and loan amounts are lower than personal credit.

In reality, credit limits on business credit accounts are notably higher than consumer cards. A business owner can secure credit cards with $10,000 limits even if their business credit score is only a few months old. This is impossible to accomplish with personal credit.

With five to 10 accounts reporting on the business credit report, a business owner can qualify for multitudes of business credit cards with limits of $10,000 or higher. A business owner can build massive amounts of business credit way faster than consumer credit.

The interest rates and incentives on corporate credit are similar to or better than consumer credit. Recently, there has been much news about the record incentives that corporate credit cards are offering to business owners. These incentives are so good that corporate credit now has higher limits and better terms than most consumer credit accounts.

Myth 3: If a company pays all its bills on time, its credit history is in good standing and strong.

Unfortunately, while paying bills on time is important, your timely payments only help your credit rating when your business works with creditors who report the payments to business credit reporting agencies.

A valuable strategy to increase business credit score is to locate and work with the vendors and merchants who work with the appropriate business credit reporting agencies. Over 90% of trade-credit is not reported to the business reporting agencies. Therefore, even if you have many accounts set up with vendors, you still might not have a business credit score or established a business credit profile.

As a business owner, you should review the credit standing of your own business, take steps to strengthen or build your corporate credit file and obtain credit with no personal guarantee or credit check.

Business Credit Benefits

1.   **Improves borrowing power**

Success in business will often be determined by whether the business has an established business credit profile and score. With a good business credit profile, the business will have an almost unlimited borrowing power. Lacking a good business credit profile, a business will have a difficult path to success, not having access to working capital and funding.

This is why, according to Dun & Bradstreet, a strong business credit file can be the difference between receiving business funds and not. Another reason for this is that approval for most small business loan decisions under $90,000 happen automatically and electronically, often relying solely on the established business credit file and score.

With an exceptional personal credit score, a good business credit score gives the business owner double the borrowing power. They can get approved for much more credit and higher funding amounts using business credit than they would if they used their personal credit to qualify.

2. Increases cash flow

Building business credit can improve business cash flow by reducing direct costs associated with financing costs, insurance premiums, vendor and supplier terms, rental terms and credit card rates. Business owners save money with lower interest rates on business loans. Moreover, they qualify for more loans, leases and government contracts.

3. Eliminates personal liability and risks

Business credit eliminates the business owner's personal liability and risk in obtaining financing. It also separates the personal credit profile from the business credit profile. Consequently, both profiles can be built to obtain greater amounts of credit.

4. Adds value and credibility

Business credit adds value to a business and gives the business genuine business credibility. Stakeholders, partners, lenders and potential buyers of the business will value the business more if it has built a strong business credit profile.

Successful companies use funding as leverage to grow their business. This is why almost all Fortune 500 companies use their business credit to secure funding; it is not that they need the money to operate.

5. Helps obtain funding without personal credit check

With a strong business credit profile, lenders will lend money based on the business's credit profile, not the business owner's. This is greatly beneficial if the owner has personal credit issues, as their business will still qualify for funding despite an impediment in their private life.

2 Chapter Two

The Three (3) Major Business Credit Reporting Agencies

The three major companies that collect and publish business credit information are Dun & Bradstreet, Experian and Equifax. **Dun & Bradstreet** is the most popular and frequently used by vendors to extend lines of credit. Property owners use them to approve office leases, as well. **Experian** is used by many credit card companies and non-traditional business lenders. **Equifax** is the most important for cash lenders such as banks. To concentrate on one and not the others is to have lopsided credibility. A business needs to build business credit with all three of these major credit reporting agencies to achieve genuine credibility.

Other business credit reporting companies, but are not big players and business owners need not worry too much about them, are PayNet, FDInsight, Business Credit USA and Client Checker.

Dun and Bradstreet (D&B)

Dun and Bradstreet is the biggest business credit reporting agency. D&B provides information on businesses and corporations for use in credit decisions. It is a publicly traded company with headquarters in Short Hills New Jersey. It trades on the New York Stock Exchange.

D&B currently holds the largest supply of business information worldwide, with over 200 million business records on file. In 2012, D&B reported that 129.4 million of these records referred to active companies that were available for risk, supply, sales and marketing decisions. Another 76.7 million were inactive companies, providing historical information for file matching and data cleansing.

D&B has a massive presence worldwide. Of the over 200 million records they had on file in 2012, they reported 54,409,439 were from Europe while 33,282,653 were from North America. A little over 12 million records were from Latin America, while more than 27 million records were from Asia Pacific. Africa only has 1,184,582 records on file. The lowest volume of records on file was in the Middle East, with 1,008,477 records on file. In total, D&B reported holding 206,148,055 records in January 2012. They also reported having over 1 billion in payment and bank experiences. In addition, they reported over 159 million public records on file.

D&B's roots can be tracked all the way back to 1841, with the formation of the Mercantile Agency in New York. In 1933, the Mercantile Agency joined with R.G. Dun & Company and became Dun and Bradstreet. In 1962, D&B created the D-U-N-S number, currently the preferred method worldwide of identifying businesses.

D&B offers many products and services to consumers and business including risk management products such as the Business Information Report, Comprehensive Report and the DNBi platform. These provide current and historical business information, which is primarily used by lenders and financial institutions to assist in making credit decisions.

D&B also offers sales and marketing products such as the DUNS Market Identifier Database, Optimizer and D&B Professional Contacts. All of which provide sales and marketing professionals with business data for both prospecting and CRM activity.

D&B is the leader in business credit data, just as Equifax, Experian and TransUnion are leaders in the consumer credit reporting arenas. Its proprietary DUNSRight Quality Process provides quality business information – the foundation of their global risk solutions worldwide. The DUNSRight process was created on the basis of four fundamental questions: is the data accurate; is the data complete; is the data timely; and, is the data globally consistent.

To answer these questions, D&B runs data through a process called DUNSRight, in which data is collected, aggregated, edited and verified daily via thousands of sources. Their ability to turn massive data streams into high quality business information is one of many factors that set them apart from any other competitor.

D&B first collects data from a variety of sources worldwide. Then, this data is integrated into their database through their very own patented entity matching system. By applying the D-U-N-S Number and using corporate linkage, they enable customers to view their total risk or opportunity across related businesses. D&B uses predictive indicators to rate businesses' past performance and assess their future risk. They are the leading provider of risk managements, business information, sales and marketing, and supply management decisions worldwide.

Dun & Bradstreet office in Center Valley, PA (built in 2006)

Experian

Experian has become the second largest reporting agency in the business credit world. They provide business credit evaluations for over 27 million small businesses and corporations worldwide. These business records are spread over 80 countries. Experian's reach is across four main geographic regions, including North America, Latin America, UK and Ireland and EMEA/Asia Pacific.

Experian's main business focus is on credit information services. These services provide insights that help businesses target new markets, predict and manage risks, and optimize customer relationships. Experian likewise offers Decision Analytics, which enable organizations with large customer bases to manage and automate large volumes of day-to-day decisions. Experian's clients include international banks, utility companies and public service providers.

Experian focuses on providing quality data and analytics to businesses to help them better assess risks. They manage a massive consumer and commercial database to help businesses obtain the best and most up-to-date information. They extract significant extra value with this data by applying their own proprietary analytics and software.

Experian diligently works to maintain their worldwide fame and growth. Their main global focus is to increase their global reach by expanding their global network and extending their capabilities into new geographic areas. They focus on innovation and on enhancing their analytics to deliver high value data to their clients. They also strive to achieve operational excellence by leveraging their global scale to deploy global products into new markets.

Experian was formerly a division of TRW, an automotive electronics giant. TRW was founded in 1901 as the Cleveland Cap Screw Company. They started producing screws and bolts, and grew to produce many parts for the aviation and automobile industry.

In the early 1960s, TRW started a consumer credit information bureau, collecting and selling consumer data, and it eventually became known as TRW Information Systems. TRW Information Systems continued compiling data and were the first to start offering consumers direct credit report access in 1986.

In 1991, rampant problems started appearing with TRW reported credit data. Thousands of people in a town in Vermont had tax liens inaccurately reported against them. Similar cases started appearing in the entire northeast, forcing the deletion of countless tax liens across the states of Vermont, Rhode Island, New Hampshire and Maine.

Dozens of lawsuits were filed against TRW, claiming sloppy procedures to create credit files, lack of response to consumer complaints and re-reporting previously deleted incorrect data. All cases were settled out of court.

TRW then created a database known as the Constituent Relations Information Systems (CRIS). This system's sole purpose was to gather personal data on 8,000 politicians who held opinions on TRW.

In 1996, TRW was purchased from Bain Capital and the Thomas H. Lee Partners for over $1 billion by GUS plc, a private group of investors. It was subsequently combined with CCN, the largest credit reporting company in the United Kingdom. GUS retained the Experian name for their combined credit services subsidiary.

In 1998, Experian also acquired QAS, a supplier of contact data management and identity verification solutions. In 2004, Experian continued its growth – purchasing Cheetah Mail, a business founded in 1998 offering e-mail marketing software and services. Because of their growth, Experian became the first company to win the UK Business of the Year award twice, in 2003 and in 2005.

Experian continued to grow in 2005 with its purchase of PriceGrabber for $485 million. In the same year, Experian acquired FootFall, an information provider for the real estate and retail property industries. Experian spent $330 million, also in 2005, in acquiring LowerMyBills.com.

In 2006, Experian made a big move when it announced its purchase of Northern Credit Bureaus in Québec, Canada. That same year, Experian demerged from their British company GUS plc, and it was independently listed on the London Stock Exchange.

Experian has continued to grow their corporation. In 2007, they purchased a 65% stake in Serasa, a leading credit bureau in Brazil. Experian continued to purchase software companies that year, including Emailing Solution, Hitwise and Tallyan.

In 2010, Experian became the first CICRA licensed credit bureau to go operate in India, where it continues to supply reports to the Reserve Bank of India's (RBI) guidelines.

In 2011, they acquired a majority stake in Computec S.A., a credit services provider in Columbia. They also purchased Medical Present Value, Virid Interatividade Digital Ltda and Garlik Ltd, expanding their data and marketing reach.

Experian's headquarters are in Dublin, Ireland. They have operational headquarters in Nottingham, UK; Costa Mesa, California, USA; and São Paulo, Brazil. Experian plc is listed on the London Stock Exchange as EXPN and in a constituent of the FTSE 100 Index. In March 2011, Experian claimed revenue for the prior year of $4.2 million. Currently, Experian employs over 15,000 people, working in 41 countries.

Equifax

Equifax is the oldest credit bureau in existence today. Since its inception, Equifax has operated in the business-to-business sector selling consumer credit and insurance reports, and related analytics, to a wide array of businesses worldwide. Equifax reports are commonly used by retailers, insurance firms, healthcare providers, utilities, government agencies, banks, credit unions, personal finance companies and other financial institutions.

Equifax provides business credit evaluations for small businesses and corporations, allowing them to detect early signs of trouble by monitoring key customers, suppliers and partners. It offers a business credit scoring model known as the Equifax Small Business Enterprise. Equifax's model is designed for companies that provide goods and services to small businesses.

Equifax sells business credit reports, analytics, demographic data and software. Its reports provide large amounts of detailed information on the personal credit and payment history of individuals and businesses to indicate how they have honored financial obligations.

Equifax's resource of data today is some of the most vital information used by credit grantors to decide what sort of products or services to offer to their customers and at what terms. Equifax's system for collecting data is NCTUE, an exchange of non-credit data including consumer payment history on Telco and other utility accounts.

Since 1999, Equifax has been aggressively growing in several other credit-related areas. It has excelled with their credit fraud and identity theft prevention products. Equifax has started earning a major part of its revenue from services that provide consumers and businesses with credit monitoring.

Today, Equifax is one of the major credit reporting agencies used in many countries. Some of the countries where Equifax is mainly used are Canada, Chile, India, Mexico, Peru, the United Kingdom and the United States of America.

Equifax was founded in 1898, about 70 years before the creation of TransUnion. Two brothers, Cator and Guy Woolford, created the company. Cator got the idea from his grocery business, where he collected customers' names and evidence of credit worthiness. He then sold that list to other merchants to offset his own business costs.

The success of this system led Cator and Guy to Atlanta, where they set up what would become one of the most powerful industries in existence today. The Retail Credit Company (RCC) was born, and local grocers quickly started using the Woolford service, which expanded rapidly. By the early 1900s, the service had expanded from grocers to the insurance industry. RCC continued to grow into one of the largest credit bureaus in the 1960s, having nearly 300 branches in operation.

Throughout the 1960s, RCC continued to provide credit reporting services, but the majority of their business came from making reports to insurance companies when people applied for new insurance policies including life, auto, fire and medical insurance. Almost all major insurance companies were using RCC to get information on the health, habits, morals, finances and vehicle use of potential clients.

RCC provided companies with services, including investigating insurance claims and making employment reports when people were seeking new jobs. In the late '60s, RCC started to compile their data onto computers, giving companies access to this data – if they chose to purchase it. They continued to buy up more of their smaller competitors, becoming larger and attracting the attention of the Federal government.

RCC began to earn a bad reputation for indiscriminately selling data, regardless of whether or not the data was accurate. They were gathering details about people, including their marital troubles, jobs, school history, childhood, sex life, political activates and more. No limit was set to the kind or amount of data they were collecting. Some of the information was factual, while large swathes were false or literally no more than rumors. RCC was said to have rewarded their employees for finding the most negative information about consumers.

When the U.S. Congress met in 1971, it enacted the Fair Credit Reporting Act. This new law was the first to govern the information credit bureaus and regulate what they could collect and sell. RCC was no longer allowed to misrepresent itself when conducting consumer investigations and their employees were no longer given bonuses based on the negative information they collected.

RCC was charged with violating the Fair Credit Reporting Act a few years later, causing even more government restrictions to be implemented. Scarred with a bad reputation for violations of the new credit laws, the company changed its name to Equifax in 1975 to improve its image.

Throughout the 1980s, Equifax, Experian and TransUnion split up the remaining smaller credit rating agencies between them, adding 104 of those to Equifax's portfolio. Equifax aggressively grew throughout the U.S. and Canada, and began growing their commercial business division across the UK. They started competing more aggressively with rivals Dun & Bradstreet and Experian.

The insurance reporting aspect of Equifax's model was phased out. At one stage, the company had division selling specialist credit information to the insurance industry, but they spun off this service, including the Comprehensive Loss Underwriting Exchange (CLUE) database, as Choice Point in 1997. Choice Point formerly offered digital certification services, which it sold to Geo Trust in September 2001.

Also in 2001, Equifax spun off its payment services division, forming the publicly-listed company Certegy, which acquired Fidelity National Information Services in 2006. Certegy effectively became a subsidiary of Fidelity National Financial because of this reverse acquisition merger. In October 2010, Equifax acquired Anakam, an identity verification software company.

Equifax has continued to grow, now maintaining over 401 million consumer credit records worldwide. They also expanded their services to direct consumer credit monitoring in 1999. Equifax is based in Atlanta, Georgia and has employees in 14 countries. It is listed as a public company on the New York Stock Exchange (NYSE) under the sign EFX.

3 Chapter Three

Business Credit Scoring

A business credit score is a mathematical model used to depict a business's risk of defaulting on an account within the next 12 months. Business credit scores reflect the likelihood that a customer will pay the merchant back as agreed. Merchants use business credit scores to help them make decisions as to who to lend money to and at what interest rate and terms.

Business credit scores are very different from personal credit scores. A business credit score reflects the business's likelihood of defaulting on an obligation, not the business owner's. Most business owners have their own consumer credit scores established. Their business also has its own score, based on how the business obligations are being paid.

Consumer and business credit scores also differ in their fundamental makeup. Consumer credit scores outline a consumer's risk of going 90 days late on an obligation within the next 24 months. On the other hand, business credit scores reflect the business's risk of going 90 days late on an obligation within the next 12 months.

Consumer credit scores range from 350 to 850, with 850 being the best. Credit scores of 800 and above are considered excellent credit. Scores of 700 and above are typically regarded as good credit, while scores of 600 reflect average credit. Consumer credit score of 500 reflect below average credit, and scores of 400 or less reflect poor credit.

Consumer scores have five main components. Each carries a different percentage of the overall credit score makeup. The largest aspect of the score relates to payment history. It accounts for 35% of the overall credit score. The consumer's available credit or their use of their accounts is the second largest score factor, affecting 30% of the overall score. The length of time the credit file has been open accounts for 15% of the overall score. The credit mix and the amount of new credit that the consumer is applying for each account for 10% of the overall consumer credit score.

Business credit scores typically range from 0 to 100, with 100 being the best. Business credit scores are based on one factor only: whether or not the business pays its obligations on time. The business's score directly reflects how that business pays.

Payment Expectation	Credit Score
Expect payment may come early	100
Payments are in early discount period	90
Payment is prompt	80
Payment comes 14 days beyond terms	70
Payment comes 21 days beyond terms	60
Payment comes 30 days beyond terms	50
Payment comes 60 days beyond terms	40
Payment comes 90 days beyond terms	30
Payment comes 120 days beyond terms	20
Unavailable	UN

The three reporting agencies who are best known for offering business credit risk scores are the previously discussed Dun & Bradstreet, Experian and Equifax. These agencies have their own unique credit scoring formula. Despite their differences, most of their score ranges remain between 0 and 100.

Dun & Bradstreet

The main credit score used in the business world is PAYDEX score. It is provided by Dun and Bradstreet. According to Dun & Bradstreet, "The D&B PAYDEX® Score is D&B's unique dollar-weighted numerical indicator of how a firm paid its bills over the past year, based on trade experiences reported to D&B by various vendors."

The PAYDEX score ranges from 0 to 100, with 100 being the best score. A score of 80 or higher is considered good or healthy credit. A business can obtain a good business PAYDEX credit score by ensuring payments are made promptly to suppliers and vendors.

D&B also offers a predictive credit score, the Supplier Evaluation Risk Rating (SER Rating). This rating predicts the likelihood that a company will file for bankruptcy and cease operations within the next 12 months. This score ranges from 1 to 9, with 1 being the lowest risk and 9 being the highest.

D&B's other supplier risk score is the Supplier Stability Indicator (SSI). This model predicts the likelihood that a supplier will encounter a large and significant financial or operational stress over the next 90 days. This score ranges from 0 to 10, with 0 being the lowest risk and 10 the highest.

Every business must first have a Data Universal Numbering System (DUNS) number before D&B will assign them a PAYDEX score. DUNS number is a business identifier code provided by D&B. They developed this business identifier code in 1963 to support its credit reporting practices.

Today, the DUNS number is widely used by lending businesses before issuing new credit. The European Commission, the United Nations and the United States government use the DUNS number. More than 50 global industries and trade associations recognize, recommend or require DUNS. The DUNS database now contains over 100 million entries for businesses throughout the world.

The DUNS number is a nine-digit number assigned to each business location in the D&B database. The DUNS number is a randomly assigned number used to identify a business.

Unlike the national Employment Identification Number (EIN), a DUNS number may be issued to any business worldwide. Certain U.S. government agencies require that a vendor have a DUNS number, as well as a U.S. Employer Identification Number (EIN).

The Office of Management and Budget, a United States federal agency, announced in the June 27, 2003 issue of the Federal Register (68 FR 38402) that a DUNS number would be required for all grant applicants for new or renewal awards submitted on or after October 1, 2003. The DUNS number supplements other identifiers, such as the EIN, and is required whether the application is made electronically or on paper.

Other agencies, such as some United Nations offices and the Australian government agencies, require certain businesses to have a DUNS number. This number is also a way in which separate corporate entities without official relationship, can be branded as one by sharing a single DUNS number among the affiliated companies.

A DUNS number is sometimes formatted with embedded dashes to promote readability such as 15-048-3782. Modern usage typically omits dashes and shows the number in the form 150483782. The dashes are not part of D&B's official definition of the DUNS number.

Numerous other business numbering systems, independent of DUNS, exist such as the International Suppliers Network system. However, few (if any) register as many international businesses as DUNS. Today, the Dun and Bradstreet's unique DUNS number is the most widely used method of identifying businesses worldwide.

Dun & Bradstreet credit reports provide access to the PAYDEX score and a great deal of other valuable information. The business's name, address and phone number are on each report, along with the business's history, incorporation date, shares of business owners and even information on directors, including resume details. D&B also lists any affiliations with that business and other businesses, other branches and subsidiaries.

D&B reports may also include financial information of a company such as known sales for the company and net worth. They list the financial condition of the company, their own rating, the DUNS number, the company's PAYDEX score and a breakdown of what it represents.

Dun & Bradstreet further lists in their reports details on payments the business has made for each individual account, including full payment record, upper-credit limit, amount currently owed on each account, amount of past due, the terms of the account and the date it was reported and last updated.

Additional information D&B provides includes detailed financial information on the business. This information might include current assets, liabilities, working capital, net worth, sales, new profit and loss, and details of actual assets and liabilities. Public record data, including judgments, bankruptcies, public filings, liens and UCC filings are also in the D&B's reports.

D&B reports list payment details for each account. Additionally, they contain detailed commentaries, indicating payment patterns, in their reports. D&B uses the following terms in their reports:

Antic indicates that payments are usually received prior to date of invoice (Anticipated).

Disc means payments are received within the trade discount period (Discount).

Ppt indicates that payments are received within terms granted (Prompt).

Slow confirms that payments are beyond vendor's terms and are being paid late.

Ppt-Slow indicates that some invoices are paid within terms, while others are paid beyond terms.

The symbol **(#)** indicates that no manner of payment was provided.

One of the most important sections of the D&B Business Credit Report is the payment summary section. Two scores in this section – the PAYDEX score and the PAYDEX score key – are critical to the report and can separate a good report from a bad one. While the two scores are related, they deal with separate issues that the business owner needs to know and understand.

The PAYDEX score is a statistical measure of a business's creditworthiness. It is the business's ability to pay its debts, very similar to a person's personal creditworthiness. A PAYDEX score of 80 is similar to that of a 700 personal FICO credit score.

A business needs a PAYDEX score of 80 to obtain the most favorable financing. This score shows that the business pay all bills on time. To obtain a PAYDEX score, a business needs at least five trade accounts reporting to their file. The business credit score itself is calculated by using as many as 875 payments.

It is important for a business owner to have those accounts report favorable payment history. If bills are paid on time, the business credit score will be positive. Conversely, if payments are made late, the PAYDEX business credit score will drop. The PAYDEX score will adjust according to how early or late the bills are paid.

How timely bills are paid, the main indicator of the PAYDEX score, is a good indicator to lenders of how likely that business is to pay its bills at an agreed upon date in the future. Lenders look at this score carefully when deciding to give a business a loan.

Another important aspect of the PAYDEX system, which most business owners are aware of, is a PAYDEX "weighted average" score. This score gives more weight to the trade accounts that report higher amounts of credit extended and less weight to trade accounts that are reporting lower amounts of credit.

This leads to a great tip. If a business owner is having any trouble meeting all their credit payback obligations, which actually means they know they are going to have to pay a bill late, it is important for that business to be sure to pay the "largest dollar" creditors first. If the business owner cannot do this, it is always best for them to contact the creditors they cannot pay and let the creditors know that they are not being ignored. The business owner should let the creditor know that they have hit a snag and will make it up to them as soon as possible, preferably even giving a date for payment.

Experian

Experian's business credit scoring model is designed for companies that provide goods and services to small businesses. Experian's business model has many names, but it is best known as Intelliscore. This model is the second most commonly used in the business world today.

Many of the largest financial institutions worldwide use Intelliscore, including over half of the top 25 P&C insurers and most major telecommunications and utility firms. Industry leaders in transportation, manufacturing and technology have also been known to use Intelliscore as their primary risk-indicating model. Intelliscore has indicators that allow for scoring depending on the business size.

Intelliscore Plus is Experian's most recent score system. It takes into account hundreds of variables. Its business score ranges between 0 and 100, with 100 being the highest. It is a percentile score that reflects the percentage of businesses that score higher or lower than the specific business being looked at. For example, if the business has a score of 20, this means that company scores better than 19% of other businesses and that 80% of other businesses score higher than that business. In performance tests, it has been found that 74% of accounts found to be risky were also in the lowest 20% of the credit score range.

Intelliscore Plus is advertised as a highly predictive score that provides a very detailed and accurate reflection of a business's risk. Intelliscore predicts a business's risk of going seriously delinquent or having a major financial issue, such as bankruptcy, within the next 12 months.

Intelliscore Plus has over 800 aggregates or factors that affect credit scores. Scores are assessed on the more than 7.2 million businesses in Experian's database. With Intelliscore Plus, Experian uses technology, such as their BizSource and True Search, for increased data depth and better matching of business records.

Experian looks at data segments such as firmographics, public records, collections and trade information. Firmographics is what Experian refers to as the background information of a business. This factor takes into account the risks inherent in the business's specific industry and the number of employees the business employs. Firmographics also takes into account the length of time the business has been reporting to Experian. Their records show that a business with a longer history of credit assessment by Experian is typically less at risk of defaulting. Inquiries are also taken into account with firmographics.

Experian places each business in one of three different models: Commercial Model, Blended/Owner Model and Intelliscore Plus. By segmenting business records this way, Experian can use more specific scoring for each individual business.

Experian provides options for reports that reflect information about the business and the business owner, called "blended" reports. They promote this as an added feature, as studies have shown that consumer reports do not offer the most comprehensive assessment of risk on their own. With blended reports, Experian takes into account the business credit score and the consumer credit score of the owner or personal guarantor. Factors taken into account are the number of accounts recently delinquent, number of derogatory payment accounts, number of accounts with 90% utilization, number of bankcards with 100% or more utilization, number of inquiries and real estate inquiries.

Intelliscore Plus, just like FICO, has multiple facets to the entire score makeup. The score is still based on the payment history of the business. However, the following business aggregates tie into the percentages of the overall score. The historical behavior, or payment history, and delinquency trends account for 5-10% of the total score. Current payment status – trade balances and percent of accounts delinquent, account for 50-60% of the score makeup. The business's credit utilization, which is the amount of credit that has been extended to the business in relation to the balances they currently have on those accounts, affects 10-15% of the total score. The company profile, comprising of the age of business, industry risk and size of business (assessed by number of employees) accounts for 5-10% of the total score. The remaining 10-15% of the total score is determined based on the derogatory items: collections, liens, judgments and bankruptcies that business has.

Model Weighting*	Business Aggregates
5-10%	Historical payment behavior, delinquency trends
50-60%	Current payment status - number / trade balance / percent of accounts delinquent
10-15%	Credit utilization
5-10%	Company profile - age of business, industry risk, employee size
10-15%	Derogatory items - collections, liens, judgments, bankruptcy

Experian credit reports contain business credit scores and summaries, and key facts about the business. Each report provides business contact information, corporate registration details and uniform commercial code filing data. Details relating to the business payment history are also included in the reports, including summaries of collections and payments, bankruptcy, judgment and tax filings, as well as banking, insurance and leasing information.

Equifax

Equifax's main business credit scoring model is the Credit Risk Score. This score was created to enhance risk assessment throughout the account life cycle by predicting the probability of a new or existing small business customer becoming seriously delinquent on supplier accounts, or going bankrupt, within a 12-month period.

Credit scores range from 1 to 100, with a lower score indicating a higher risk of serious delinquency. By definition, the score predicts the likelihood of a business incurring a 90-day severe delinquency or charge-off over the next 12 months.

Scores of 90 and above means that obligations are being paid as agreed. Scores from 80 to 89 indicate payments are being made 1-30 days overdue, while scores of 60 to 79 represent payments being paid 31 to 60 days past the agreed-upon due date. Credit scores ranging between 40 and 59 indicate payments are made 61 to 90 days overdue, while scores between 20 and 39 mean obligations are being paid 91 to 120 days overdue. Scores between 1 and 19 mean obligations are being paid 120+ days past the due date.

Equifax also provides a business credit score for suppliers, known as the Small Business Credit Risk Score for Suppliers. This model is designed to help credit grantors improve their risk assessment and reduce delinquency rates to help improve profitability. In addition to the supplier, Telco and utility credit history, the score utilizes unique bank loans, lease information, credit card, public records and firmographic data from their own Equifax Commercial database.

The Small Business Credit Risk Score for Suppliers' credit scores range from 101 to 816, with the lower score indicating a higher risk. If the business had a bankruptcy on file, they would have a zero (0) score. There are four major factors affecting the score: the number of years the business has been in business, the evidence of judgments or liens, and the length of time since the oldest financial account was open on the report and whether the business has a 45% or higher trade utilization ratio.

Equifax offers a Business Failure Risk Score with many reports. This risk score predicts the likelihood that the business will fail or file for bankruptcy within the next 12 months. This model helps identify businesses that pose a greater risk for failure so suppliers and credit grantors can take appropriate actions.

The Business Failure Risk Score takes into account information gathered from supplier trade information, firmographics and public record information from Equifax's Commercial database.

Business Failure Risk Scores range from 1000 to 1880, with a lower score indicating a higher risk. With this, a zero (0) score indicates the business has filed for bankruptcy. The Business Failure Risk Score provides up to four reason codes to point out the top factors that affected the score. Unlike other risk scores, this unique score indicates the likelihood that the business will cease to exist within the next 12 months.

Equifax provides many details on each business for which it produces credit reports. Each report has a profile of the company with the business name, address and phone numbers. Inquiries the business has made into other credit are also displayed, along with the business's credit score. Each report also lists the Risk Score and key factors affecting that score.

On the reports, Equifax provides a payment index explaining the credit score breakdown. There are even graphs that track the business's current utilization and the number of days the business paid beyond the given terms.

Public records information and a credit report summary section are displayed. Information on the number of accounts, the length of time the credit has been active, the number of charge-offs, total past due, the most severe status within the last 24 months on any accounts, the single highest credit extended, the total current credit exposure, and the median and average open balances on accounts are also in the said section.

Additionally, Equifax reports show any recent credit activity for the business and financial information such as information on business cards, loans and other credit extended by financial institutions. The reports also show the amount of credit usage and reflect any trending that Equifax has identified.

Equifax reports provide many details for each financial account listed on the business report. The account number and current account status is listed.

Moreover, each account shows the date the account was last reported on, the date it was opened and the date the account was closed. All financial accounts listed on Equifax reports show the current credit limit for the account, the balance owed and a full 24-month payment history.

Equifax reports details on non-financial accounts. These details include account number, account type, date reported and date opened, date of last sale and the payment terms, the high credit and current credit limit, the account balance, past due amount and aging categories. Public record accounts report the registered name, filing date, incorporation date, incorporation state, status, registry number, and contact name and address.

Each Equifax report has an additional information section with alternate company information including DBA names, addresses, phone numbers and the parent company, if applicable. In this section, the report lists guarantor information, comments from the business owners or credit grantors, and recent inquiries.

4 Chapter Four

How to Build a Strong Business Foundation

The perception lenders, vendors and creditors have of a business is critical to the business's ability to build strong business credit. Before applying for business credit, you must insure your business meets or exceeds all lender credibility standards. In total, over 20 credibility standards are necessary for a business to have a strong and credible foundation.

When building business credit, everything matters. The exact number of employees claimed on the application is sometimes the basis for approval. In other cases, a business credit application might be denied if the business did not claim the right amount of vehicle gas usage in a month.

Avoid using certain types of phone numbers. It is essential to ensure your number is listed in places the business credit reporting agencies and creditors will look at. If a business does not have the right type of phone number, or if it is not listed in the right places, the business will most likely be denied credit.

The type of corporation you list, the years your company has been in business and the type of ownership all factor in to getting a business APPROVED for higher credit limits. Most importantly, knowing and understanding which of the thousands of creditors to apply to and in which order to apply are essentials in the business credit approval process.

The first step in building business credit is all about establishing credibility for the company. You should think about the approval process from a lender's perspective to improve chances of approval. Lenders are in business to lend to companies they consider "safe risks". They will be doing a number of underwriting checks to see if the business is "safe" enough for them to consider extending credit.

Part of establishing the business as a safe risk is complying with lenders' standards for approval. Being in compliance helps the business establish credibility, and it is an important foundation for success in business credit building.

Business Fundability

Business Fundability is essential in getting approved for business credit. "Business Fundability" is a phrase coined by those in the lending industry to describe how a business measures up in relation to the entire business lending and investing community.

Fundability is not just about business credit. It includes several components that determine how lenders, investors, insurers and suppliers see the business overall. The business is worth the risk for the business owner, but is it worth the risk for the lender? The answer will increasingly be "yes" as the business fundability grows.

The major components of Business Fundability include business bank accounts, business assets, business revenue, and the owners and their business's credit history. By improving the fundability your business, you are truly improving the overall "health" of the business while greatly increasing its ability to succeed now and in the future.

Every lender follows their approval guidelines when considering a loan application. Here are a few of the main items that typically get a business denied when trying to build business credit and obtain financing:

- no 411 directory assistance listing
- bank account balance rating of "low 5"
- having fewer than 5 trade credit accounts reporting to credit bureaus
- not having a credit file number
- business credit scores below 70
- debt coverage ratio higher than 5:1

Many conventional banks that offer funding require extensive documentation for a client to qualify. The required documentation includes:

- interim financial statements
- most recent Federal Tax Returns for each principal owner
- accountant-prepared financial statements including Profit & Loss statement and Balance Sheet for the last 3 years
- personal financial statements for each principal owner

- Organization papers such as incorporation papers, DBA papers, business licenses etc.
- list of business and personal assets that can be used as collateral
- names and contact information for at least three credit references

These documents can be very difficult to supply if you have a start-up business, all the more if you have never done any business before. Many banks expect your business to be established before you request financing. However, it is possible for you to get started even without having an established business.

Building a Strong Foundation

One of the first aspects of an application a lender will look at is the business name. A business must use its exact business legal name. The full business name should include any recorded DBA filings the business is using. A business must also insure the business name is the same on the business corporation papers, all licenses and bank statements.

One can build business credit with almost any type of corporate entity. If the business owner truly wants to separate business credit from personal credit, their business must be a separate legal entity, not a sole proprietor or partnership.

Unless they have a separate business entity (Corporation or LLC), they might be "doing business" but are not truly "a business". A business must be a Corporation or an LLC for its business credit to be truly separate from its owner's personal credit.

Business credit cannot and does not exist for a sole proprietor. All that a sole proprietor has available are personal loans or lines of credit. This credit is tied to the business owner's personal social security number.

Every business entity must have a Federal Tax ID number, also called **Employer Identification Number (EIN)**. Without an EIN, a business entity cannot apply for business credit, whether that business has employees or not. An EIN does for a business what a social security number does for a business owner as a person. This number identifies the business to the Federal government and IRS.

EIN is used to open business bank accounts and to build the business credit profile. A business owner must take the time to verify that all agencies, banks and trade credit vendors have their business listed with the same tax ID number.

A business must be a brick-and-mortar business to look credible to most lenders. The address must be a real deliverable physical address. The business address cannot be a home address, a PO Box or UPS address. Many lenders and merchants will not approve a business for credit unless this criterion is met.

There are a few popular solutions for business owners who might not have a real, physical address. One of those solutions is an "Address only" virtual office. With this, a company that offers virtual office solutions provides each of their clients a proper business address, which the clients can use. They receive their client's mail and packages at their real, dedicated address; then, they forward them to wherever their client chooses.

Another business address solution is a "Virtual Office". With this type of office, the business has a real professional business address and a dedicated phone and fax number. This service often comes with receptionist services, and it sometimes includes part-time use of fully furnished offices and meeting rooms.

A "True Office" is a real office a business owner can rent. The business will have its own full-time private office with receptionist services, dedicated phone and fax, Internet, full furnishings, meeting rooms and other amenities.

With any of these solutions, a business can create the perception that it has a big office in a major city even if in reality it could just be a one-person home-based business. This boosts a business's image and can help increase a business's chance of being approved for more credit or getting higher-limits on the approved credit.

A business must also have a dedicated business phone number that is listed in the 411 directory to appear credible to most merchants and lenders. The listing in the directory assistance should be under the exact business name.

A Regus office building in Herndon VA

Lenders, vendors, creditors and even insurance providers will verify that the business is listed with 411. A toll-free number will give the business credibility, but the business must have a LOCAL business number for the listing with 411 directory assistance. Lenders perceive 800 numbers or toll-free phone numbers as a sign of business credibility. Even if the business owner is a single owner with a home-based business, a toll-free number provides the perception that the business is a bigger company.

It is easy and cheap to set up a virtual local phone number or a toll-free 800 number. No business owner should ever use a mobile phone or home phone number as their main business line. This can get the business flagged with the business credit reporting agencies as "un-established" and high-risk business.

Lenders perceive a credible business as one with a fax number. Business owners need a fax number to receive important documents and to fax in credit applications to lenders and merchants. With e-faxes, which can be set up very affordably, you can receive and send faxes through email.

Having a company website is to a business's advantage. Credit providers will research the company applying for credit on the Internet. It is best if they learned everything directly from that company's website. Many places online offer affordable business websites, so a business can have an Internet presence that displays an overview of the company's services and contact information.

Every business also needs a professional company email address. Setting up a business email address is too easy and affordable for a business owner to neglect. When a business sets up its email address, it is essential that they avoid using free email services like Yahoo and Hotmail. There is nothing worse than credit providers seeing an email address like dallascowboyfan@gmail.com. The email address should be @company.com. A great example is an email like support@mycompany.com or john.doe@company.com.

The business's banking history is vital to its future success of being able to secure larger business loans. The day that many lenders consider the business to have become operational is the date the owner opened the business's bank account. Therefore, if the business incorporated 10 years ago but opened its business bank account just yesterday, then, that business started yesterday. The longer the business banking history, the better the borrowing potential will be.

One of the most common mistakes when building credit for a company is non-matching business addresses on the business licenses. Not having the necessary licenses for your type of business to operate legally is worse. Every business owner needs to contact their state, county and city government offices to see if there are any licenses or permits required to operate their type of business.

Business owners must also ensure that state business filings are listed correctly; county or city license and/or permit filings are listed correctly; and, IRS filings are listed correctly. Business owners must also confirm that every agency, creditor, supplier and trade credit vendor has their business listed the exact same way.

A business must be listed with the exact same spelling of the business name and the exact same address and phone number. For example, one might have you listed as "ABC, Inc.", while another has "AB Consultants, Inc." and another as "AB Consultants". There are also simple differences like those between "Suite 400", "#400" and "Apt. 400". Business owners should correct such differences.

Every business owner should take the time to verify that main agencies (state, IRS, bank and the 411 directory) have their business listed the same way and with the exact legal name. In addition, they should take the time to ensure every bill (power, phone, property owner etc.) has the business name listed correctly and delivered to the business address.

Business owners must file all applicable business tax returns to have a credible foundation. There cannot be any unfavorable public records for the business including no liens, judgments or lis pendens against the business. Many lenders will also want to see a business model when the business is applying for higher amounts of funding.

5 Chapter Five

Business Credit Reports Made Easy

A business starts building a brand new credit profile in much the same way a consumer does. It starts with no credit profile. Then, it is approved for a new credit that reports to the business credit reporting agencies.

The business uses the credit and pays the bill in a timely manner. As the business has established a positive business credit profile, and as the business continues using the credit and paying the bills on time, it will qualify for more credit.

The first step in business credit building is for the business owner to order a credit report for the business. It is very important for the business owner to know what really is being reported for that business in regard both to positive and negative information. The business owner will also want to actively monitor the business credit building and score building as it is taking place.

Business Credit Reports

Many business owners find, when they receive their Business Information Report from D&B, that they have a low PAYDEX score. They scratch their heads and wonder why their score is low even when they are paying the bills on time.

Without having a credit report, a business owner cannot find out which companies are reporting negative information to their file. However, they can obtain a list of all the companies that are reporting to the business credit file. Upon request, they will get a list of all the companies reporting to the business credit bureau as well as the number of times they reported. The PAYDEX score will also be on the report.

To get the list, a business owner can call a D&B representative and ask them for the list of companies reporting on their business. There must be at least five companies reporting before the representative will be able to pull this list.

An overview of the companies that have reported and the dollar-weighted payments are on page 2 of the report. Each of the companies listed will be sorted by supplier industry. If there are less than 20 companies on the list, the D&B representative might choose to simply read the list over the phone or e-mail the information to the business owner.

Other information on this report includes the total dollar amount of all trades reported, the largest amount that any one trade has reported and the percentage of payments that have been made to the top 10 industries.

A business owner will first want to get a copy of their business credit reports to see what is being reported in Experian, Equifax or D&B.

The Experian Smart Business credit report reflects the number of tradelines reporting. It also shows whether the business credit score has been assigned, the business has an active Experian Business Profile, and the business has had any recent credit inquires. For a copy of their Smart Business report from Experian, business owners can visit http://www.smartbusinessreports.com/. As of writing, the charge for a single report or credit monitoring is $49 to $99.

An Equifax Small Business Credit Report can be obtained here: http://www.equifax.com/small-business/credit-report/en_sb. It typically takes more time to create a file with Equifax Small Business than with D&B or Experian. Their full reports currently cost $99.95.

Obtaining a D&B number (D-U-N-S #) begins the process of building a business credit profile with Dun & Bradstreet. The D-U-N-S # will also play an important role in enabling the business to borrow without a personal guarantor. D&B's website is http://www.dnb.com/. Depending on the type of credit report package one gets, a report can cost between $299 and $699 per DUNS Number.

D&B also offers their DNBi Self Monitor to monitor business credit during the building process. A subscription for D&B Self-Monitoring is about $39 to $99 per month depending on the add-on options a business owner might choose.

Once a business sets up its credit report and pays bills on time, it should have a high PAYDEX score. It is vital that the business maintains its report.

The business owner should check the business report periodically. They may want to consider purchasing the Monitoring Service that D&B offers. This service allows a business owner to receive alerts when new positive or negative information appears on their report. A business owner will be notified of changes in the following areas:

- Credit Rating
- Suits, liens or business judgments
- PAYDEX score changes
- Changes to financial statements
- Other significant business news

D&B reports may contain some errors. A business owner should review their business report. Most problems needing resolution will be dealt with through the eUpdate website. However, major issues will need special attention. In those cases, it is best to pay

D&B to get an account representative to fix the problem quickly and efficiently so that it does not affect the owner's business file.

It is extremely important that the business credit file remain accurate. The Fair Credit Reporting Act does not apply to businesses as it does with consumer reports. If there is something wrong on the business credit report, or if a step is skipped in setting it up, there is no legal recourse to have that information removed. If the file was set up incorrectly, there is a good chance the business credit file could be put in the "High Risk" category, making it nearly impossible to remove inaccuracies.

6 Chapter Six

Building Vendor Credit Made Easy

A business credit report can be started in much the same way as a consumer report commonly is – with small credit cards. The business can be approved for small credit cards to help it build an initial credit profile. These types of initial cards in the business world are commonly referred to as "vendor credit".

A vendor line of credit is a line of credit that a company (vendor) extends to a business on *Net 15*, *Net 30*, *Net 60* or *Net 90 days* terms. This means that the business can purchase their products or services up to a maximum dollar amount, and the business owner has 15, 30, 60 or 90 days to pay the bill in full.

Therefore, if the business owner is set up on Net 30 term and was to purchase $300 worth of goods today, then that $300 is due within the next 30 days. With vendor accounts, business owners can get products and services for their business needs and defer the payment on those for 15 days or more, thereby easing cash flow.

Some vendors will approve the company for Net 30 term upon verification of as little as an EIN and a 411 listing. It is important that business owners always apply first without using their SSN. Some vendors will request it, while some will even say on the phone that they need to have it, but it is best to submit first without it.

Vendors are the "Gate Keepers" of business credit. They are the REAL secret of business credit building. One of the main reasons that 90% of business owners do not have access to business credit is because they do not know where to go to get VENDOR ACCOUNTS to build their business credit profiles and scores.

A business owner can go to Home Depot today and apply for business credit. However, they would typically be denied, or approved with a personal guarantee. To be approved by Home Depot with no personal guarantee, their business must first meet the business credit qualifying requirements. The problem is most people do not know what their qualifying criteria are.

A business owner cannot just walk into a merchant, such as Wal-Mart, Staples or Home Depot, and be approved for business credit with no personal guarantee. They first must have a good business credit score, and five or more tradelines reporting on their business credit to be approved.

Here is where most people get stuck. They cannot get credit since they have no business credit, so they are never able to build their business credit. The real secret to business credit is vendor accounts. With these accounts, a business owner can be approved for credit with vendors who will report to the business reporting agencies. This makes it easy for a business owner to build five or more trades and establish an excellent score.

A business will need to start with "preferred vendors". These are vendors who are known to extend credit to all businesses, even those with no credit history. Remember when I said in the early part of this book that it takes 90 to 120 days to a build business credit score? The credit reporting cycles are the main reason for that, and it cannot be done faster.

When the first Net 30 account reports as "tradelines" to D&B, the DUNS system will automatically activate the business credit file if it is not yet activated. This is also true for Experian and Equifax.

A business needs at least five vendor accounts reporting on the credit to be truly established. If these accounts are paid promptly, an excellent business credit score will be established. With these new accounts and score, a business will be able to start getting approved for revolving credit accounts.

It is important for a business owner to know that some vendors require an initial prepaid order before they can approve a business for terms. It is also essential that every established vendor account is being used and paid promptly in full.

Business credit building is much faster to do than consumer credit building. Still, it does take some time, and a business owner must be patient and allow time for the vendors' reporting cycles to get into the reporting systems. It typically takes three cycles of "Net" accounts reporting to build a credit score.

This means it could take as long as 90 days between the initial payment to the merchant and the account report on the business credit report. It does happen faster, within 30-60 days, but it can take as long as 90 days or three reporting cycles.

Once the accounts are reported, a credit history is begun. The business will then have a business credit score based on how the bills were paid – on time, early or late. As more and more accounts are added to the credit report, more tradelines are established, and the credit profile becomes "deeper".

Merchants who offer higher limits and revolving credit cards will want to see "deep" credit profiles. They will want to see a business credit report that has many tradelines being paid as agreed or early each month.

To be approved for more accounts, the business needs to have reporting trades with higher credit limits. Many merchants who offer revolving credit cards want to see a business credit profile that has many tradelines, and some of those trades should have limits of $10,000 or more. As the business has more accounts reporting as paid as agreed, other vendor sources will approve the business for higher credit limit accounts.

Vendor sources are not easy to locate. This is one of the main reasons very few businesses have established business credit. Most business owners look for reliable sources who will offer them the initial vendor credit they need to start building a business credit profile but cannot find such sources. Those who do find another major challenge: They lack knowledge and understanding of what it takes to be approved with each resource.

Most merchants who offer vendor credit do not promote that they do so, and they certainly do not make underwriting guidelines public. Therefore, if the business owner does find some vendor sources, the next challenge is for them to know enough about the underwriting guidelines to be approved. This causes frustration because many businesses apply for initial credit to build their credit profile, but they are denied for reasons unknown.

In the business world, lenders and merchants do not need to disclose why they deny credit to a business. This is unlike the consumer industry, where this information has to be provided to the consumer – including the credit bureaus that were pulled to make the decision to disapprove. This has always been one of the biggest challenges with building business credit. Owners do not know where to apply and what the guidelines are. When they are denied, they are rarely provided any details to help them correct their issues so they will be approved when they reapply.

In this book, I will provide many sources that can be used to build vendor credit. These sources are like gold when it comes to business credit building. They are the secret to getting approved for the initial tradelines to start building business credit, to establishing a positive business credit score and to start getting approved for revolving credit card sources.

Starter Vendor Credit Sources

The following accounts are perfect starter accounts for business credit building. They are great accounts because they work for most businesses, including startup businesses.

1. **Radio Shack**

One vendor that is great for business credit building is Radio Shack. It is one of the nations most experienced and trusted consumer electronics specialty retailers. Radio Shack offers products most business owners need and want such as computers, phones, batteries, cables and connectors.

Radio Shack is one of those creditors who report to D&B and Experian. It will pull a business credit report to see how the business had paid bills in the past. If there is not enough data on the business credit report, Radio Shack will ask for bank and trade references. This will start the reporting process for a business and place the business on the radar of other lenders.

To be approved, most businesses need to have been in business for at least two years. In addition, they must have a DUNS number and credit references. Like most vendors, Radio Shack offers payment terms of Net 30 for their vendor accounts. Currently, you can call 1-800-442-7221 to get an application. Fill it out, and fax back it back to 817-415-3909.

2. **Quill**

Quill sells office supplies, cleaning supplies, packing and shipping supplies, school supplies, printing supplies and more. From filing and storage to hand-held computers, Quill has a wide range of discounted top-name brand products.

Quill reports to D&B. Typically, they require that a business place its first order before being considered for a Net 30 account. If the business has established a D&B score, it will probably get approved with the initial order.

For new businesses with little to no credit history, the business will probably be put on a 90-day prepayment schedule. If an order is made every month for 90 days, they will more likely approve a Net 30 account. New businesses can start out with smaller limits that will increase when bills are consistently paid on time.

3. **Laughlin Associates**

Laughlin Associates will make sure your business is in corporate compliance with all documents, including Articles of Incorporation, Corporate Minutes, Corporate Resolutions and List of Officers.

Laughlin Associates will approve any business listed in 411, and has a business bank account and an EIN. They report all payments to Experian. It takes 30 to 60 days for the first tradeline to show up on the credit report from the date of purchase. They offer low monthly payments, and they report as a Net 30 account.

4. **Monopolize Your Marketplace**

    Monopolize Your Marketplace offers a marketing system that teaches businesses about how to market their business. They provide 10 audio CDs and over 11 hours of materials that focus on marketing topics, including the marketing equation, MYM technology, industry category strategies, the master marketing letter and more.

    Monopolize Your Marketplace is a great starting vendor, as they will approve most businesses for at least $400 vendor credit. They report accounts to Experian and offer Net 30 terms. They offer a payment plan for their system and report the payments they receive to Experian. To be approved, a business needs to have an EIN, a real deliverable address and a business bank account.

5. **ITC Web Services**

    ITC offers many web and technical services, including website creation. They offer affordable websites and will even revamp a business's current website. They provide Joomla, Drupal, PHP and MySQL website development.

    They also help businesses create professional email addresses, web applications, flash animation design, logo design and web banner design, and develop mobile device apps.

ITC Web Services is another great starter vendor source because it reports to all three business credit reporting agencies. They offer a vendor account with Net 30 term.

ITC Web Services will approve a business for a vendor account without a personal guarantee from the business owner, and they do not require a personal credit check on the owner. However, they do require a business to be listed in the 411 directory and to have a business bank account and an EIN.

6. **Business Marketing Services**

    Business Marketing Services does custom website creation, social media marketing, search engine optimization, logo creation and more. It offers a Net 30 starter vendor credit account and reports to Experian and D&B. Business owners must provide a valid proof that their business is operating in the U.S. for them to be approved. Business Marketing Services usually requires 30% payment upfront on purchases and extends credit for the other 70% of the purchase paid over a 5-month period to almost all businesses.

7. **Market Click Internet Marketing**

    Market Click Internet Marketing offers online services, such as search engine optimization and setting up websites, for maximum online exposure. They report to D&B and offer Net 30 terms.

    Market Click Internet Marketing gives business credit without requiring any personal guarantee from the business owner and rarely requires a personal credit check. It takes them about 30 to 60 days to report the tradeline to D&B.

8. **A Printer 4 U**

A Printer 4 U offers graphic and logo design services, printing, banner creation and much more. They give most businesses, even startup businesses, and a Net 30 credit line of up to $2,500. They report to Experian and D&B. Often, they require a 50% payment upfront on all orders; the business can then finance the rest.

A Printer 4 U requires the business's phone number to be listed in the 411 directory. They also ask for the address, phone number, bank account information and trade references of the business. They require no personal guarantee, and they will approve businesses with no personal credit check from the business owner.

9. **Paramount Payment Systems**

Paramount gives businesses the ability to offer payment terms to customers on their products and services. They will accept customer checks from a business, front the business the money from that check, then charge a fee to the customer to collect on those checks; there is no recourse for the business owner if their customers' checks do not clear. With this system, Paramount gives business owners access to funds right away.

Paramount offers Net 30 terms and reports directly to D&B. They do not do business with some industries, such as web design, jewelry, used cars, online businesses, and some basic retail stores. To be approved, a business must provide an EIN and two years of credit references. They must also show proof on how long they have been in business.

Other Vendor Credit Sources

Many other available vendor accounts come from very well-known companies. However, most require a minimum number of years in operation or established tradelines to qualify such as the following:

1. **Staples**

    Staples, a mega-retailer that sells office supplies and offers business services, offers a Net 30 reporting business credit tradeline that reports to all three business credit reporting agencies.

    Staples will check with Experian, Equifax and D&B to see if the business has a credit history. The amount of money they approve a business for depends on the business's established credit history. If the business has no or little credit history, the business owner will typically be asked for a personal credit check and personal guarantee. Staples will also check if the business is listed in the 411 directory and has an EIN.

2. **ULine Shipping Supplies**

    ULine Shipping Supplies is one of the leading distributors of shipping, industrial, packing and janitorial products. They offer a vendor account that can be used for business credit building. This account is offered on Net 30 term and is reported to D&B.

    ULine requires every business to have a DUNS number before they can be approved. They will look at the business credit report, searching for existing tradelines, and they might require trade and bank references. They normally want to see at least two trade references and one bank reference.

    If they pull a business credit report and see little to no credit history, they will require a few orders from the business to be prepaid before they will offer their Net 30 account. They might also ask for the business's financials.

3. **Home Depot**

Home Depot is one of the world's largest retailers for home and building supplies. They offer a vendor business credit account on Net 30 terms, and reports to Experian and D&B.

To be approved, the business must have an EIN. It must also have been in business for at least three years. If it has been open for three years or longer, Home Depot most likely will not ask for a personal guarantee from the business owner or require a personal credit check. However, they will require a personal credit check and guarantee from the business owner if the business has been open less than three years.

4. **Grainger Industrial Supply**

Grainger Industrial Supply is a popular credit source that thousands of suppliers use for electrical fasteners, fleet maintenance, HVACR hardware, material handling, pneumatics, power tools, pumps and more. They offer a Net 30 account that is reported to D&B quarterly.

If the business has a business license, they will be approved for $1,000 account or less. If the business has trade and bank references, it will be approved for accounts over $1,000. They will require the business to provide an EIN.

5. **Labor Ready**

   Labor Ready is a leading multinational source of dependable labor for companies across many industries. They offer a vendor account on Net 7 terms and reports to D&B. They require a valid tax ID number and will approve a business for Net 7-day account with no personal credit check or personal guarantee required from the business owner.

6. **Sherwin Williams**

   Sherwin Williams offers a Net 20 vendor account that reports to D&B. They offer a wide variety of products ranging from coatings for plastics, metal and wood to many industries. They will pull both personal and business credit for approval and will typically approve a business with an established, strong credit profile with Dun & Bradstreet.

7. **Macy's**

   Macy's is a large department store that can supply business with many of the things they may need for employee recognition programs, dress code programs, and special holiday and thank-you gifts. Their vendor account is offered on Net 30 terms and is reported to D&B.

   Macy's will only approve a business for their vendor account if the business has a positive D&B credit score established. They will compare the business score against the industry average score to determine approval. They require no personal credit check or personal guarantee from the business owner, but they normally request bank.

8. **Budget Car Rentals**

Budget Car Rentals accounts are reported to Equifax and Dun & Bradstreet, and are approved as Net 30 terms. A business must already have had a Budget Express Account for at least two years and spent over $5,000. For approval, the business must also be listed in the 411 directory and have at least 20 employees.

7 Chapter Seven

Building Revolving Credit Made Easy

For the best business credit-building success, a business should obtain at least five revolving business credit card accounts and five vendor accounts. These accounts report to the business credit agencies in different ways and carry more weight than the vendor credit that was initially used to start building the business credit.

After five tradelines have been established and reported, the business will be able to start getting approved for revolving business credit accounts. A revolving credit account is one that allows the business to pay a minimum due per month and not the full outstanding balance. These accounts normally report to Experian, D&B and sometimes Equifax. Because of how they report, these accounts will help build business credit on a larger scale than the Net 30-day vendor accounts alone do.

Once a business owner has obtained a total of 10 reported accounts, including vendor and revolving accounts, it can then start qualifying for real credit cards through Visa and MasterCard. Of the 10 open accounts, at least one account should have a credit limit of $10,000 or more to qualify for Visa and MasterCard credit.

Most major merchants offer business credit. Many of these accounts offer credit limits of $10,000 or more. A business can get multiple Visa, MasterCard and AMEX cards, and it can continue increasing its limits.

Within a few months of starting the business credit building process, the business will qualify for thousands of real useable credit. Within 6-12 months, the business will have access to over $50,000 in revolving credit with major retailers. Depending on how it utilizes its newly acquired credit, the business can continue to qualify for $100,000 to $250,000 in a year or two.

A business can also secure $50,000 to $150,000 credit lines based on business credit with limited income document requirements. With full income verification, around $250,000 credit lines are available. Most of these credit lines come with check-writing capability and a linked debit card.

Revolving Credit Sources

Many merchants offer revolving credit accounts for businesses. Some of these accounts are starter accounts. These starter accounts are very useful to businesses that are still in the early stage of building their business credit, including those with only a few vendor accounts reporting as tradelines on their business credit. Other accounts might have more stringent requirements for approval than basic starter accounts have.

1. **Staples**

    While the business owner's application is on hold, Staples will verify if the business has an EIN and if it is listed in the 411 directory. They will also check to see if the business name and address match the 411 listing. They will check that the business credit files are open with D&B and Experian.

    For businesses with established business credit, they will not require a personal guarantee from the business owner. If no business credit is present with Experian or D&B,

Staples will do a credit check on the business owner and will require a personal guarantee.

2. **Dell**

Business owners visit Dell to buy computers and accessories for their home or business. The Dell Business Credit Account is a popular revolving line of credit that provides an easy way to finance purchases of Dell equipment and reports to D&B.

Dell regularly approves accounts with limits up to $10,000, usually to business owners with PAYDEX score of 75 or higher. However, a business must have been open for at least six months before they will approve that business. They will sometimes check personal credit during their approval process.

3. **Lowe's**

Lowe's offers a huge selection of tools, kitchen appliances, cabinets, cabinet hardware, countertops, paint and much more. Customers can purchase online or at their local Lowe's center. It is a popular source of revolving business credit accounts and reports to D&B and Experian.

Lowe's offers a fast online approval. Applicants with a DUNS number can apply online for approval. They are typically approved for credit limits between $1,000 and

$5,000. Unless a good D&B and/or Experian score is established, businesses that have been open less than three years will require a personal guarantor. If the PAYDEX credit score is over 85, they will normally approve the business for credit of $5,000 or more.

Lowes will approve a business for business credit with no personal credit check or guarantee from the business owner so long as the business has been open for over three years. If the business has a strong business credit profile and score, they might also approve the business with no personal guarantee required.

4. **Office Depot**

Office Depot is another mega-retailer that provides office products, office supplies, office furniture etc. Their revolving account reports to both Experian and D&B.

Office Depot will check the business's credit profile with Experian or D&B before approval. If one business credit reporting agency has no or little information reported, they will check the other credit agency's report. If the business has little to no credit report with either, a personal guarantee from the business owner will be required. Even if a personal guarantee was provided, this account will be reflected in the business credit reports, not in the personal credit reports. The amount approved will depend on the business credit scores they pull. They might also request trade references if there is no business credit score, or if there is limited credit reporting.

5. **Wal-Mart**

Wal-Mart is one of the best-known retailers in the world. They offer a massive assortment of products, including electronics, toys, home, garden and baby products.

Wal-Mart's account is revolving and reports to both Experian and Equifax. A business should be approved for this account if it has some business credit already established with Equifax and D&B. Wal-Mart requires a business credit score of 75 or higher, reflecting that the business pays its obligations as agreed each month. If the business cannot be approved due to limited credit, it can get approved with a personal guarantee from the business owner.

6. **Costco Wholesale**

Costco Wholesale is an international chain of membership warehouses. They offer an American Express business account with revolving terms that reports to D&B.

Costco looks at the business credit of the business and the personal credit of the business owner with all three credit reporting agencies. Moreover, the business must have an EIN, and the business owner must provide a personal guarantee if the business has been open for less than two years.

7. **Amazon.com**

Amazon.com is an online shopping company that sells books, magazines, music, videos, electronics, computers, software, apparel and accessories.

They offer their revolving account with no personal guarantee to businesses with an EIN, provided that the business has been open at least three years. They report to Experian, Equifax and D&B.

Depending on the amount of business credit the business already has established, Amazon issues credit limits ranging from $500 to $2,500.

8. **Sears**

Sears sells a wide variety of products, including appliances, lawn tractors and tools. Their business credit account reports to all three business credit reporting agencies.

They require good business credit score for approval, and they look at business credit score from D&B. If there is no score with D&B, they will check with Experian and Equifax.

They do not require a personal guarantee from business owners with established strong business credit score. In addition, a business must have been open for at least two years and must have an EIN.

Business Credit Gas Cards

Major fuel companies around the country are great sources for business credit gas cards. Business owners can use their gas cards for fuel purchases. These accounts are especially good for truck drivers and other businesses that have vehicles on the road as part of their business model.

1. **BP**

    BP offers a business credit card that reports to D&B and is a revolving credit account. This card can be used in more than 12,500 BP stations around the globe. It can be used for a business fleet's fuel and maintenance needs anywhere MasterCard is accepted.

    To apply, a business needs to provide its tax ID number. BP will look at Experian, D&B and Equifax scores. If the business has strong credit profiles and scores, it can be approved with no personal guarantee from the business owner – as long as the business has been open for at least three years.

2. **Chevron**

    Chevron also offers a great business gas card that is revolving and reports to D&B. Chevron business gas card can be used at both Chevron and Texaco stations to purchase gasoline, tires, batteries and more.

    A business needs a PAYDEX credit score of at least 75 and must have been in business for at least 18 months to be approved with no personal credit check or personal guarantee from the business owner.

3. **Speedway Super America**

    Speedway Super America's business credit gas card is revolving, and it reports to Experian and D&B. To be approved, the business must have been in business for at least a year.

4. **Sinclair Oil**

Sinclair Oil also offers a gas merchant account. It is a revolving account that reports to D&B. The account can only be used at Sinclair stations. No personal guarantee or credit check is required from businesses with established business credit history and positive scores.

5. **CSI**

CSI offers a corporate fleet MasterCard account that is accepted at nearly every retail and diesel CSI fueling location. It has over 180,000 stations nationwide. This account is revolving, and it is reported to Experian and Equifax.

CSI requires that 10 accounts be reported on the business's credit reports before they will approve a business for a revolving business credit account. It also requires that one of the tradelines have a credit limit of at least $10,000 before it will approve that business for credit.

CSI requires the business to have an EIN and to present all required business licenses, a copy of a voided check, a copy of a utility bill that shows the business address and phone number.

Other Merchant Credit Sources

Before they will approve a business for a revolving business credit account, the following merchants require the business to have an EIN and to present essential documents: all required business licenses, a copy of a voided check and a copy of a utility bill that shows the business address and phone number. Additionally, they require that 10 accounts be reported on the business credit reports.

1. **Sam's Club**

    Sam's Club is a warehouse retail chain that offers office supplies, business furniture, vending items, cleaning supplies, paper products, food service supplies, computers and more. It offers a revolving business credit account that reports to Experian and D&B.

2. **Key Bank**

    Key Bank offers a MasterCard credit account. With this account, a business can earn points that can be redeemed for airline travel, merchandise, gift certificates and more. They offer a 0% introductory rate for the first 6 months. This revolving account reports to Experian, Equifax and TransUnion.

    Key Bank requires that one of the business's tradelines has a credit limit of $10,000 or higher before they will approve that business for credit. They will request a personal credit check and guarantee from the business owner if the business does not match these conditions.

3. **Volvo**

    A Volvo MasterCard is offered through Wright Express (aftermarket support). It is a great revolving business credit account. This account reports to both Experian and Equifax.

    Before a business will be approved for credit, Volvo requires that one of the business's tradelines has a credit limit of $10,000 or higher. The business must submit its financials for it to be approved with no credit check or personal guarantee from the business owner.

4. **Fleet One Local Fuel Card**

If a business uses cars, vans or trucks, the Fleet One Local Fuel Card is a great business credit solution for them. This account is offered on Net 14 terms and reports to all three business credit reporting agencies. This card can be used to pay for vehicle fuel and maintenance.

The Fleet One Local Fleet Card requires that one of the business's tradelines credit limit is $10,000 or higher before they will approve that business for credit. They will request a personal credit check and guarantee from the business owner if the business does not have the required number of tradelines and credit limit.

8 Chapter Eight

Know Your Bank Ratings

It is essential that business owners separate their personal bank accounts from their business bank accounts. This is vital in running a successful business. A separate business bank account helps business owners keep track of their business transactions such as deposits, withdrawals, wire transfers, issued checks etc. This makes maintaining accurate records and preparing financial reports easy tasks for them.

Business owners should select a bank that can best cater to the needs of their business. While every bank offers various types of financial business products, each serving a specific need, one thing remains the same throughout - bank credit.

Bank credit is the total amount of borrowing capacity a business can obtain from a banking system. This is not the same as business credit, which is a much broader category of lenders such as suppliers, credit card issuers or leasing companies.

A business can secure more business credit quickly as long as it has a bank reference and an average daily account balance of at least $10,000 for the past three months. This yields a "bank rating" of Low 5 (an ADB of $5,000 to $30,000). This rating is based on the average minimum balance maintained in the business bank account over a three-month period. A lower rating, a High-4 for instance, will not put a stop to the business's application, but it will slow down the approval process. Most banks assume the business has little ability to repay a loan or a line of credit if they have a rating poorer than Low 5. Therefore, before a business applies for credit, it should keep a balance rating of Low 5 for the past three months.

Business owners should do whatever they can to keep at least $10,000 in their business account for over a 90-day period. The money should be kept there to ensure the bank rating is high enough to increase future financing approvals. It is also essential that business owners ensure that their business bank accounts are reported exactly the way all their business records are, with the exact same physical address (no P.O. Box) and phone number.

It is vitally important that every credit agency and trade credit vendor, every record-keeper (financial records, income tax, web addresses and e-mail addresses, directory assistance), also lists the business name and address the same way. No lender is going to stop to consider all the ways a business might be listed when they look into the business's credit worthiness. If they cannot find what they need easily, they will simply deny the application.

It is essential that businesses manage their bank accounts responsibly. Businesses should avoid writing non-sufficient funds (NSF) checks at all costs, as it destroys bank ratings. It is a good idea for the business to add overdraft protection to their bank account as soon as possible to avoid NSFs.

It is also very important that businesses show positive cash flow, where the amount of cash coming in their bank account is higher than the amount going out of it. When the account shows a positive cash flow, it indicates that the business is generating more revenue than is used to run the company.

It is also important to recognize that banks are motivated to lend to businesses with consistent deposits. Thus, a business owner must make regular deposits, more than the withdrawals they are making, to maintain a positive bank rating. Consistent deposits coming into the business bank account are looked upon very favorably.

Bank credit is not only based on the monthly deposits, balance rating and check history of a business. It also includes the age of the business's account, the bank products it uses and any savings account or investments the business has.

A seasoned bank account shows stability and longevity in the eyes of lenders. Keeping a healthy and long standing relationship with a bank is also crucial for all companies. A good, stable relationship with a bank reflects longevity, and it is highly appreciated by lenders.

A business should consider working with a financial institution that specializes in providing banking services tailored to their specific industry. Working with a lender that already understands the business makes getting a loan approved much easier than working with those who do not because majority of lenders have difficulty assessing the credit risk of small businesses or industries they know little about. It is much easier for a lender to underwrite the business's financial risk when it truly understands and specializes in making loans to a business in an industry they are familiar and comfortable with.

9 Chapter Nine

How to Get Business Funding

In lending, when lenders look to see if a client is fundable, we are looking for one of the 4 C's. Your business does not need all of the 4 C's; it only needs one to secure funding.

The 4 C's of Business Lending

The first C is **Cash Flow**. When your business has good cash flow, it can qualify for business funding. Your business's verifiable cash flow substantially increases your chances of being approved for business funding.

If your business does not have cash flow, it still might have **Collateral**, the second C. Collateral for a business is really the business assets. Many things can be used as collateral including equipment, purchase orders and even account receivables. Having Collateral greatly increases the chances of a business being approved for funding.

If your business does not have Cash Flow or Collateral, it can still qualify for business funding. Lenders also look at *Business* **Credit**, the third C. Lenders will lend money without personal guarantee based on the business's credit profile and score. If the business has a good business credit profile it can use that as security to obtain funding.

If you have not established business credit, call me. I can help you quickly build an excellent business credit score and profile.

Maybe your business is just starting, and it does not yet have business credit, cash flow or collateral. You can still qualify for funding. Lenders will use your **Personal Credit**, the fourth C, to qualify the business for funding. Credit lines up to $250,000 are available today even for startup businesses with personal credit scores as low as a 650 FICO. These types of unsecured credit lines do not look at revenue or financials. The business owner's personal credit is all that is used to qualify for funding.

Secured vs. Unsecured Funding

It is easier to be approved for secured funding. Even if business owners have credit issues, they can still obtain many types of secured funding. This is because *secured funding* requires something as collateral for the funding the business receives.

When you own a business, you have business assets that you can use as collateral to obtain funding. Equipment financing, for example, leverages equipment as collateral for the debt. On the other hand, purchase order financing uses purchase orders as collateral, while account receivable factoring uses receivables as collateral. Real estate can be used as collateral, and so can revenue. Since these financing options are using an element of the business as security, personal or business credit does not have to be great to qualify.

With good business credit, a score of 650 or higher, a business owner can also qualify for unsecured funding options. **Unsecured funding** is where the bank will lend money or approve for a credit line with no security required. Business owners do not need to leverage any aspect of their business as collateral. The lender will base the lending decision on the quality of the business credit profile or the business owner's personal profile. With a good business credit profile built, a business can qualify for large amounts of business funding.

Interest rates on unsecured debts are higher than secured debts, as the lender's risk is higher. Still, a business owner can obtain good working capital loans and credit lines at very reasonable interest rates and payments.

Secure Money Before It Is Needed

In lending, most applications are denied when the applicant is in need of money the most. Lenders lend based on risk. The better a business is doing, the lower the risk it is from a lender's prospective. Most business owners do not look for money until they need, sometimes desperately, it.

Maybe it is as simple as an AC unit going out or a freezer breaking. Something usually happens that costs much more than what is on hand. This is the worse time for business owners to be looking for money. Major problems can be fixed without even a little hiccup if money is sitting and waiting.

Business owners should investigate and obtain business credit and funding before they really need it so that when a business owner runs into a BIG problem, the financial solution is available. This credit can be grown to even greater amounts over time and can be secured without a personal guarantee.

Most business owners go to their bank when they need money. As many entrepreneurs are now discovering, banks have greatly tightened up their lending guidelines making it harder than ever to be approved. For this reason, business owners should check for possible financing from companies that offer multiple finance options.

The truth is there are billions of dollars ready to lend right now for small businesses. However, much of the available funding cannot be secured through a conventional bank. Factoring companies, credit unions, merchant companies, private and angel investors all have money to lend to you right now but, if you do not know exactly what type of financing you need, it is tough to know where to look.

For example, most business owners do not know about Business Revenue lending, Purchase Order, Account Receivable Financing, Equipment Leasebacks or Merchant Advances. Most banks do not offer these types of financing options. Unless a business owner knows exactly the type of financing they are looking for, they will not know these options exist.

10 Chapter Ten

Business Credit and Funding Is Available

The main reason most business owners build their business credit is to gain access to revolving credit accounts and cash funding. There are many sources that will give businesses funding based on their business credit. Those sources offer an abundance of different funding options to help businesses meet their financial needs.

Most business owners tend to rely on their bank when funding is needed. The problem with this is that banks only have access to limited financing options. Moreover, most of the financing options banks offer check out all the business's financials, revenues and assets, and the business owner's personal credit and assets.

Most banks only offer SBA-insured loans. This means the only business loan products they offer require full documentation from the business owner, including financials, profit and loss statements, bank account statements, tax returns for 2-3 years, good personal credit from the business owner, and good business credit.

If a business does not have all these things, most banks will not approve them. Moreover, even when a business does supply all these documents, they must show little or no issues for the business to be approved. Therefore, if there is an NSF on a bank statement, or a particular year does not show a lot of net profit, the business might be declined for most business funding programs.

Many other forms of funding available for businesses are not offered through banks. Many of these types of available financing will not look at all the business financials, or the assets or personal credit of the owner, or even the revenue and business assets. They only focus on certain aspects of the business and not the entire business itself.

Many of these programs do not require all the financials and documentation that full document SBA programs require, and they are easier to qualify for. Therefore, it is essential that business owners work with those who can offer their business many financing options and not just the limited sources that banks offer.

In this chapter, I will talk about many of the programs that you might not have heard of before. Knowing these programs exist is the very important first step towards getting approved.

Credit Lines

Unsecured revolving business credit lines are a smart way to grow and expand a business. The business owner pays only the credit they use; this makes revolving credit lines a perfect financing source for most businesses. In addition, revolving business lines can be used, paid down, and then reused making them very practical for business owners. Knowing that additional money is available if needed gives business owners tremendous peace of mind.

The amount a business will be approved for varies depending on the volume of business being done. A business owner can secure a revolving credit line for over $150,000 with no financials needed to qualify and credit lines up to $250,000 if they are willing to supply their business tax returns and financials.

Some revolving lines require collateral be put up to qualify. Collateral can include accounts receivables, inventory, machinery and equipment, and even real estate. Other credit lines are available with limited to no financial documents needed to qualify.

Most business revolving credit lines require a personal guarantor to be approved. This means that if the business owner fails to meet the terms of the agreement the personal guarantor will be liable. With a strong credit profile and score built, a business can qualify for business revolving credit lines without the owner needing to provide a personal guarantee.

Most banks have cut back dramatically on the funds they are offering to small business owners. As a result, many owners have found it very difficult to obtain revolving business credit lines.

Brand new startup businesses with no financials can qualify for credit lines up to $150,000. There are no financials required for many of these types of credit lines, and the lender will not even look at the business's monthly revenue. However, most lenders want a strong business or personal credit profile for these types of credit lines.

If the business does not have a score and credit profile built, the lenders will want to look at the personal credit and will require the business owner to supply a personal guarantee. If a strong business credit profile and score are built, the business can be approved without a personal guarantee from the business owner. The better the personal or business credit is the higher amount the credit line approval will be.

With most of these credit lines, the business owner can use someone, such as a friend or a relative who may or may not be associated with the business but has good credit and is willing to be liable in case the payments are not paid, as a Personal Guarantor if the owner has credit issues. The lender could pursue the personal assets of that friend in case the business owner defaulted on payments of the credit line.

These credit lines are some of the best accounts in the country for new startup businesses and new franchises. The business owner will receive a debit card and/or a checkbook, so they can write from this account. It only takes 2-4 weeks to close and have the money in the business's bank account.

Equipment Financing

One of the best and smartest ways to obtain the equipment for a business is by using equipment financing. A business owner can deduct the interest paid on the lease and not need a large down payment to be approved. This is one of the reasons over 80% of U.S. businesses use equipment lease financing to acquire equipment for their businesses.

Using equipment financing, business owners can improve business cash flow and increase capital. They can keep their normal cash flow, leave their money in the bank, avoid major out-of-pocket expenses incurred by purchasing the equipment upfront and benefit from multiple tax advantages.

Equipment Leasing is one of the most common types of equipment financing available today. When leasing equipment, a business owner will find that most leasing options offer fixed-rate financing. This means the interest rate and payments will stay the same from month-to-month during the term of the lease.

Whether the business needs office equipment or large commercial equipment for manufacturing, equipment financing is a perfect solution for the business. Equipment financing can also be used for someone who is just starting a new business and needs equipment to operate.

Typically, the lender will collect 1-2 of the monthly payments upon approval. This amount of money required is usually equal to 3-7% of the total equipment cost. The business owner will have low monthly payments. These payments can be tailored to fit the company's individual needs. Taxes and other charges, such as installation charges into new equipment leases, can be included.

Equipment loans are perfect for any business owner looking to purchase equipment.

Merchant Cash Advances

A business owner can get money for their business quickly by borrowing against future credit card sales. This type of financing is known as merchant cash advances. These loans use past and current credit card history to determine how much financing to grant a business.

Merchant loans can be obtained up to $150,000. These loans are available for businesses that process as low as $3,500 monthly in credit card transactions. The higher the processing volume the higher advance loan the business will be approved for.

Money is advanced to the business based on how much credit card transactions it processes each month. A small portion of each future credit card sale goes towards paying back the merchant advance loan, not interfering with the business's cash and check receipts. It has no fixed repayment amounts or terms, which gives flexibility to the business if it is having a slow month.

One of the best benefits of merchant advances is that the business can receive money in its bank account as soon as 24 hours after approval. Another great benefit of merchant loans is that the business owner does not have to have good personal credit to qualify. These loans leverage positive credit card processing history for approval, not the business owner's personal credit score. Although it has some credit score restrictions, a business can be approved with even below average personal credit score in most cases. Moreover, no personal guarantee is required, and no collateral is needed.

Every business has its strengths and weaknesses. If a business uses credit cards as a payment source for clients, a merchant advance can be the perfect way for that business to obtain a lot of money in a short period.

There are no application fees and no out-of-pocket costs. Funds can be used for any purpose, including payroll, marketing, increasing business inventory, paying taxes, paying rent, advertising, ordering supplies and equipment, expanding the business, opening an additional location or using the funds for working capital.

SBA Financing

One U.S. Small Business Administration (SBA) program that might be perfect for many businesses is known as **CAPLines**. This loan program helps small businesses meet their short-term and cyclical working-capital needs. CAPLines has many types of lines of credit, including seasonal lines, contract lines, builder lines, and standard and small asset-based lines.

Each line has a separate purpose that can help the business and its owner. For example, the *Standard line* is a revolving line of credit for cyclical growth, recurring and short-term needs. The *Seasonal line* can be used to offset lower revenues in slower seasons, while the *Contract line* can be used to pay for contract costs for expansion.

The SBA also has a great loan program called the **Microloan Program**. It provides small, short-term loans to small businesses. Some of the common uses for Microloans include working capital, the purchase of inventory or supplies, the purchase of furniture or fixtures, and the purchase of machinery or equipment. Terms, interest rates, and fees vary based on the size of the loan, the planned use of funds, the requirements of the intermediary lender and the needs of the small business borrower.

Small Business 7(a) loans are well known and loved in the business community. If a business is awarded a 7(a) loan, the loan proceeds may be used to establish a new business or to assist in the acquisition, operation or expansion of an existing business.

The SBA has decided to give U.S. veterans and military members funding incentives and special programs such as the Patriot Express program. This is for veterans and members of the military community wanting to establish or expand small businesses. The SBA and its resource partners offer counseling and training to supplement this loan initiative, making it more accessible and easy to use.

Eligible military community members include:

- Veterans
- Service-disabled veterans
- Active-duty service members eligible for the military's Transition Assistance Program
- Reservists and National Guard members
- Current spouses of any of the above
- The widowed spouse of a service member or veteran who died during service or of a service-connected disability

Loans can be used for many purposes. Some of the most common purposes are:

- Start-up costs
- Equipment purchases
- Business-occupied real-estate purchases
- Inventory
- Infusing working capital

- Managing the business
- Expansion
- Preparing the business for the possibility of the business owner's deployment
- Setting up to sell goods and services to the government
- Recovery from declared disasters

Patriot Express loans feature the SBA's lowest interest rates for business loans, generally 2.25% to 4.75% over prime depending upon the size and maturity of the loan.

SBA has an express program to expedite loan approvals. The SBA *Express* program gives small business borrowers an accelerated turnaround time for the SBA to review the loan application. Applications can be approved within 36 hours. In addition, lower interest rates are often available when the application is submitted through this *Express* program.

Purchase Order Financing

Seasonal sales, business growth and expansion, and large orders can all restrict a business's cash flow. Many consumers want to pay on terms of net 30 or 60, but many suppliers demand payment on delivery.

At the same time, the business has to cover other expenses, including shipping, labor costs, materials, packing and so on restricting cash flow further. Purchase order financing helps free up business cash flow, so the business can grow and profits can soar.

A business can obtain funds based on outstanding purchase orders with existing clients. While a bank looks at the company's finances, these loans focus on the financing and credit of the business's customers. This means this type of financing can be obtained even if the business owner has personal or business credit issues.

Different purchase order financing options are available. One option is to obtain funds that are paid directly to suppliers. A business owner can receive advances up to 100% of the purchase cost to their supplier. The lender will pay the supplier, and the business owner receives immediate access to the goods.

The lender will collect the invoice payments from the client and will pay the balance between the order value and the amount paid to the supplier. The business owner receives the net total minus any fees once payment has been received.

A second purchase order financing option is to issue a Letter of Credit to the business suppliers. This letter is a commitment to pay the supplier on their fulfillment of certain conditions. The conditions are normally related to the supplier providing necessary documentation. These Letters of Credit are also governed by the regulations of the International Chamber of Commerce.

A third option is a Supplier Guarantee. This is a commitment to pay the supplier from the availability generated on the funding of the receivables when generated relating to the purchase transaction.

The amount of purchase order financing available for a business will depend on the volume of outstanding purchase orders they have. It is very practical to obtain over $500,000 in financing if the business has that amount or greater in orders. Some purchase order financing climbs as high as $20,000,000 or higher in funding.

Funds can commonly be delivered within a week after approval, and interest rates and terms are typically very good.

Revenue Lending

A great way for businesses to access money is through revenue-based financing, sometimes referred to as revenue participation or revenue sharing funding. Revenue financing is a loan to a company that is paid back through a royalty on the revenues. Typically, this royalty is in the 2% to 5% range.

With revenue-based capital, instead of selling ownership in the company, the owner sells rights to a percentage of the business's revenue for some period. Funding is commonly available up to 25% of the company's annual revenue. Money is received monthly, sometimes equal to 10% of monthly revenues. To qualify, a company must have current revenue.

One of the benefits of revenue funding is that it provides a variable payment. If revenue for the business goes down, the loan payment also goes down. This is extremely helpful in seasonal industries.

Revenue financing typically has no collateral requirement. Unlike bank loans, it does not require personal guarantee. In addition, there are no restrictive covenants. This funding can be used for many purposes, including growth capital.

Inventory Financing

Inventory financing is a bank line of credit secured by the company's inventory as collateral. With inventory financing, the borrower receives a loan in order to purchase inventory. The purchased inventory is then used as collateral against the loan.

This is a great finance option for business owners as it provides the inventory that a business needs without tying up cash, receivables, credit cards or bank lines. This type of financing can help free up some of the cash tied up in inventory for more pressing needs. Inventory loans are perfect for businesses that enjoy a high inventory turnover rate but are short of the cash needed to replenish their supplies.

Inventory financing loans are also convenient for businesses that need to keep some capital free for other interests and investments. Lenders will typically need to see that a business has a proven sales history to be approved. In addition, they will require the business to have tangible inventory.

Lenders will want to see that the business has a proper inventory management system in place, which provides accurate and timely information on the business's inventory size and cost. To be approved a business owner should ensure that the inventory is protected from damage and shrinkage. Most lenders will also require sales orders to verify the business is actively selling.

401(k) Financing

Business partners can borrow against their 401(k)s to obtain funds for their business. To start setting up 401(k) financing, a business will first adopt a retirement plan. Specifically, the retirement plan should be a profit-sharing plan that allows 100% of the plan assets attributable to rollovers to be invested in employer stock.

Business owner can quickly and easily rollover their retirement funds from their previous employer or IRA into the new 401(k) plan. The funds can come from multiple different sources and multiple people, including their spouse or an employee who is looking for an investment opportunity.

In addition, thanks to provisions in the tax code, this can be done without a penalty. By rolling funds into retirement financing, the owners can buy a small business or use funds for their existing business, or use funds as an investment inside their retirement plan without distribution penalties.

A few of the many benefits of retirement financing include:

- Utilize funds from retirement accounts like IRAs, 401(k)s, 403(b)s, Keoghs, SEPs etc. without incurring early distribution taxes or penalties

- Start a small business with minimal to no debt while securing significant tax benefits

- Use up to 100% of retirement funds, or use a portion as a down payment on an SBA or unsecured loan

- Save thousands in interest fees and protect personal credit
- Lower business overhead while aggressively growing the business owner's retirement account

Wrap Financing

Wrap financing is for business owners who want to "wrap" their vehicles with graphics. "Wrapping" turns a vehicle into a mobile billboard.

Many business owners swear by this marketing technique and insist it brings them significant amounts of business. Most business owners do not know that they can obtain financing to wrap their vehicles or even the windows in their business.

Wrapping a vehicle sometimes costs upwards of $2,500. Nevertheless, with financing available, this makes it much more affordable for business owners.

Signage Financing

Commercial signage can be expensive. To have a company install a sign in front of one's business, especially a lighted sign, can cost thousands of dollars.

Many companies skimp on their signage due to the huge cost of commercial signage. However, business owners do have the ability to finance their signage.

Private Investors

Many private investors are currently hungry to invest money into make-sense projects. These investors will gladly offer loans for many projects when most banks will not. This gives a business owner a great opportunity to secure the money they need to grow their business, even if their bank has said no.

Receivables Financing

Receivables financing or "invoice factoring" is a great way to get money for a business. Accounts receivable financing is not a loan; it is an advance against client invoices. The business is selling outstanding invoices to a factoring company who then gives back up to 95% of the invoice value in the form of a loan against those invoices.

Receivables financing is mainly used to generate immediate cash flow for the business selling the accounts receivable. It is a great funding option as it provides an immediate advance of cash to a business leveraging its outstanding invoices. This means that the amount of funding the business will qualify for grows as the business grows, so it can meet increasing demand. This is why most major companies, including most Fortune 500 companies, use some form of accounts receivable financing.

One of the best benefits of receivable financing is that the business receives an increase in working capital without needing to borrow money, or tie up business or personal assets. This boost to cash flow positively affects profitability. Money can be received quickly, typically within 24 hours from approval. This is much faster than if the business was trying to collect on the invoices on its own.

Prior to purchasing invoices, a factor conducts a credit analysis on the client being invoiced to determine their risk on repaying the invoice. The business owner is entitled to the resulting analysis, which is a huge benefit as it can assist the business owner in their future business dealings with that client.

Another big benefit of receivable financing is that the business is not obtaining a loan. This is not considered a loan since the business is literally selling its own receivables. A business can be approved for as much as $25 million in financing.

It is easy to qualify for since the cash advanced is based on the client's credit status, not on the business owner holding the receivables. A business may qualify for factoring even if it is a new company without an established record of accomplishment, has a tax lien or has declared bankruptcy. Accounts receivable financing really boosts cash flow by providing an immediate advance of cash into the business against the value of the business's outstanding invoices.

Angel Investors

Angel investors can be your saving grace when looking for business funding. Sometimes, angel investors are willing to lend money when other banks and financial institutions simply will not. Interest rates and fees with angel investors can also be very favorable, sometimes better than bank rates and terms.

Even though angel investors are a great source of business funding, there are some things to be cautious about before committing with an investor. Despite their name, angel investors are not there to rescue the business. These investors are usually businesses or individuals who have money to lend but expect to take a safe risk and earn a nice return on their investment.

These investors are usually one-time investors. Many angel investors do not lend to the same person twice, even if that person paid them back perfectly. They choose to spread their risk out over many people and many businesses to insure they get a safe return on their investment.

Another concern with angel investors is that they typically want a percentage or part of the company. They may want a small stake, or full control and 51% ownership.

When the angel investor wants a stake in the company, it is important that the terms are acceptable for the business owner as well. The investor's funds can help grow a business, but the trade-off of handing over part of the company means the deal has to be worth it for the business owner as well as the angel investor.

An additional concern with angel investors is that they sometimes commit but do not follow through, and close on the transaction. For this reason, it is essential that the business owner not spend any of the funds until the deal is completely done, and the funds are in the bank. Nothing is worse than committing those funds only to discover that the deal falls apart and the angel investor never delivers the funds.

Securities Based Loans

Securities based loans are an excellent source of funds for someone who holds publically traded stocks. Securities based lending generally involves a revolving line of credit that uses eligible investment portfolio as collateral.

This funding option permits a business owner to access funds without immediately liquidating their portfolio. This gives them the ability to access liquidity while maintaining their portfolio's current exposure to the market. The business owner continues to receive the benefit of any dividends, interest or capital appreciation that may accrue in the account.

Some of the other main benefits of securities financing include:

- Interest rates range from 2.5% to 4.5%, fixed, interest-only payments

- Loan periods up to 10 years

- Funds may be used for virtually any purpose, anywhere in the world

- Borrower's nationality and residence can be anywhere in the world

This loan is non-recourse and non-recorded. The lender cannot come after the borrowers personally nor report them to the credit bureaus in case of non-payment. The business owners get to keep the money if they default, while the lender gets to keep the stock as the sole remedy.

At the end of the loan period, the borrower will receive back from the lender the same number of shares originally pledged as collateral, which automatically includes any appreciation as well. This is a great option for many business owners, especially foreign nationals and borrowers with limited or undocumented income. No credit check is required, so even those with challenged credit may qualify.

Private Equity

Private equity financing is money that is invested in a privately held business in exchange for partial ownership of the business. The invested funds might come from private individuals or institutional investors.

Private equity financing often involves large amounts of capital even though there is no set limit of how low or high the investment can be. Despite the fluid nature of this type of financing, a business will have to meet some criteria in order to obtain this type of business funding.

The investors will look for assurances that their money will be used wisely and in a way that increases the likelihood that the investment will bring higher returns than would be expected if giving business loans.

The investor will balance the risk of investment loss again the possibility of investment gains then make a decision as to whether the risk is manageable.

The investor will investigate if the entrepreneur assumes more risk exposure than the equity partners or investors. They will check the stage the business is at: a startup or a well-established business looking to expand. They will want to know how much experience the management has in the industry, the size of the investment request, the company's history (including its historical financial and market performance), and how it compares to the size of the business.

The investor will also check to see if there is a quality business plan with realistic goals and projections, if there is a complete marketing plan, and if the business is willing to accept investor restrictions placed on the investment.

Private equity investors can set their own unique requirements and restrictions for business funding, and business owners must be willing to agree with them. The good news though is that business owners have more negotiating leeway since this is private funding and not financial institution lending.

Though companies have been experiencing difficulties getting approved for business loans in the current economy, private equity financing has always been available. Unfortunately, many business owners simply do not know how to go about finding or raising this type of fund.

Crowdfunding

Crowdfunding is a great financing source for new startup businesses with a limited budget. Crowdfunding is the process of getting funding from a community instead of an individual or finance institution. The network pools their money and resources to support the new business.

Crowdfunding enables the "small guys with big ideas" to secure funding to start their endeavor. Those who are starting a business can post their project idea to the community. If the community sees your project and idea as promising, they give out the necessary funding without any interests or collateral.

Crowdfunding originally started as a way to help generate funds for charities. It then became popular for artists, including street performers, before becoming a viable funding option for other small businesses. In 1997, the British band Marillion even funded their entire tour through crowdfunding. Since its original inception, a very diverse group of entrepreneurs has been using this funding vehicle.

Crowdfunding investors do not require any principals returned or interests paid. With some crowdfunding, the business owner offer something in return for their supporters' money. Millions of supporters are active in crowdfunding communities with money to lend.

The average loan amount is smaller. On average, loan amounts are below $25,000. In many cases, loans are for smaller amounts of $5,000-10,000. Crowdfunding is perfect for entrepreneurs who do not have a standard business model that fits with normal funding. It is also perfect for new business owners who have great ideas and only need a little money to get going.

Credit Cards

It can be quite a challenge for a small business owner to decide which business credit card is the best for the business owner and the business. When looking for the best types of card for the business, an owner will first want to know about the different types of business credit cards that are available today.

A **business debit card** is a card that works like a business checkbook because the limit is the amount of funds the business currently has available in its business checking account. Whenever the business owner uses the card to make a purchase, the amount charged is deducted right from that account.

A **prepaid business card** is a convenient alternative to carrying cash and works just like a secured consumer credit card. Funds are added to the account and whatever amount is added is available to use for purchases.

A **secured business credit card** is specifically designed for businesses with no credit or less than perfect credit history. An initial security deposit is required, which establishes the card's credit limit. In most cases, a minimum deposit of $500 is mandatory and once the business owners begin making purchases they will receive invoices like a regular credit card.

An **unsecured business credit card** works just like a normal, revolving, and unsecured consumer credit card. Depending on the issuer, credit limits are based on many factors. It can range from personal credit and/or business credit ratings to years in business and annual revenues. An *unsecured business credit card* gives the business the opportunity to earn incentives and rewards.

A **business charge card** has all the convenience of a credit card without the high interest rates. When using this card, the business owner will have to pay the card balance in full each billing cycle. Because they cannot carry a balance, a charge card does not have a periodic or annual percentage rate, so there is no rate for a charge card issuer to disclose.

If the owner plans to pay the balance off each month, a card offering travel mile rewards or cash back bonuses may be the best business credit cards. If, on the other hand, they plan to maintain an ongoing balance, a low introductory or standard APR might be a better option.

Remember, just because a card issuer offers all kinds of benefits and rewards, it does not mean it is necessarily the best card. A business owner should always read the fine print to understand the terms and conditions, and fees associated with the card completely.

It is also important to note that even though business credit cards are not covered under the new CARD Act certain issuers are extending the CARD Act protections to its card holders.

11 Chapter Eleven

Personal Credit Matters

This book covers a lot of information about how to build business credit for a business. However, this book would not be complete unless it included a chapter also covering how personal credit works as personal credit plays an important role for any business that is applying for funding. This is essential to help you understand business credit better.

Many business credit sources will approve a business with no personal credit check. This means a business can secure a lot of credit, including store credit cards and other credit from Visa, MasterCard, even American Express. However, most funding that includes loans, credit lines, and even merchant advances will require some kind of credit check from the lender. In most of those cases, the lender does not make the lending decision based on the personal credit. Nevertheless, to insure the business owner is not currently having financial issues, lenders look at the owner's personal credit.

Your Credit Quality of Life

It is easier to understand business credit fundamentals when you have a good background of what credit is, and how the consumer credit system works. Credit is an agreement between a creditor or lender and a borrower in which the consumer assumes something of value in agreement to repay the creditor based on certain terms.

Car dealers, banks, credit card companies, mortgage companies, signature loan companies, pay day advances, and even student loan agencies are a few of many sources who extend credit to individuals.

When a person goes to apply for new credit, these creditors review the person's credit profile to determine the individual's risk of repaying that debt. Based on their risk, they are approved or denied credit. If they are approved, the repayment terms will (again) be based on the quality of their personal credit profile. The better the personal credit profile and the higher the consumer score, the better terms the borrower will receive.

Consumers with bad credit profile will be charged higher interest based on that risk. The rate of interest varies based on many factors, but interest charges can be significant. One credit card company in 2009 even released a credit card with an 89% APR!

Importance of Credit

If you have ever been denied a loan or a job due to your credit profile, then you already know the importance of your credit profile in your life. From the payments consumers pay each month to whether they can rent or own their dream home, most are affected by a person's credit quality.

Home loans, rent, car payments, credit cards, installment loans, car insurance, cell phones, health and life insurance, and monthly utilities are all based on the quality of a consumer's personal credit. In addition, many employers are now checking their prospective employee's personal credit profile to help make hiring decisions. Thus, between those who have bad and those who have good credit profiles, a dramatic difference in their quality of lives is evident.

Life with Bad Credit

People can live even if they have credit issues. However, those issues can cost them tens of thousands of dollars each year making it hard to survive and near impossible to save money for their future.

Many consumers do not have the extra money to save due to paying tens of thousands of dollars each year in outlandish interest charges. This is one of the fundamental reasons the U.S. savings rate has stayed under 1% for four years through 2007.

I have spent more than a decade of my life in the finance industry. I have done thousands of financial reviews with clients. Most had no idea how much their credit was really costing them.

Sure, they knew that bad credit was causing issues with them getting approved for new credit. However, in reality, my clients (like most consumers), did not REALLY know how much credit affects their day to day lives.

Bad credit ruins lives. The difference between living a good life and struggling to survive is greatly affected by a person's credit quality. With a bad credit profile, credit cards, utility, insurance, and so many other regular family expenses cost more.

Let us look at a car as a simple example. There are around 250 million car owners in the U.S. alone. Chances are you are one of them, or you know someone who is. Many car owners chose to finance their vehicles and pay monthly payments until they pay off the debt.

Car loans are offered to consumers based on their credit history and credit score, like most other loans. Based on those credit factors, auto lenders determine the risk and establish the interest rate and total amount payable.

With good credit, consumers get a longer term and better interest rate. With bad credit, they will pay much greater interest on a shorter term. Thus, a $20,000 car loan with good credit will cost approximately $322 monthly -- based on a 5% interest rate for 72 months. The exact same $20,000 car loan with bad credit will cost approximately $541 monthly -- based on a 21% interest rate for 60 months.

One is costing $219 more EVERY month. That is a total of $9,276 difference. The consumer with bad credit will pay 46% more than the one with good credit. These examples are not extreme. These are based on common interest rates a consumer will actually see on a $20,000 auto loan.

Rent and home expenses are another area where customers are taken for great amounts of interest. A $100,000 mortgage costs a good credit consumer $577 monthly and $207,720 over 30 years. The same home would cost a family with challenged credit $841 monthly and $302,760 over 30 years.

The consumer with good credit will pay $264 less per month and save $95,040 over the lifetime of the loan. That means the person with bad credit will pay $95,040 more in interest for a $100,000 loan due to their credit.

The Bad Credit Trap

What most people do not know is that bad credit can control their lives. With bad credit, outrageous amounts of extra interests and higher monthly payments are charged each month forcing them to live from paycheck to paycheck. If an emergency arises, many consumers in this position are heading for total financial catastrophe. With bad credit, their lives are just like a house of cards waiting to collapse.

Consumers with credit issues do not have high open limits to use in case of emergencies. When a transmission goes out or a child needs emergency dental treatment, payday loans become the only option to get money in a pinch. The rates on those are extremely high making them almost impossible to pay off.

I call this the **Bad Credit Trap**. Most consumers will never get out of out of this trap. The system will not allow them to recover naturally.

In my career, I have heard many clients tell me how good their credit was, and then it went bad. However, I have never had even one client with good credit tell me their credit was bad and it magically got better.

Most with bad credit never recover. That is a fact. The reason is that the system is against them from the start. More often than not, consumers with credit issues are not in their situations because they are bad people. They were sucked into the bad credit trap, which they simply do not know how to get out of.

Credit problems usually stem from an uncontrollable event. Some have a car crash or medical issue that compiles medical bills. Many others go through divorce or have credit too young, leading to issues where a default or late payment occurs.

When one account is paid late, a downward credit spiral begins. Even if the late payment was just for one credit card, most other card companies will claim their risk is higher. Then, many creditors will lower their limits. If a creditor lowers the credit limit on an account, the credit score goes down because 1/3 of a person's credit score is based on their available credit. The consumer ends up with less available credit, right when they obviously need it. With lower available credit, they will face more overdraft fees. Their credit score drops, and risk increases for all other accounts due to the lowered score.

Consequently, creditors will start to increase interest rates due to the increased risk. Not all creditors can do this, but in the fine print, many reserve the right to do just that. The higher rates mean the payments also increase. The consumer is now faced with having to pay higher on several of their accounts, in addition to their original late fees.

Eventually, this leads to the consumer going late on other payments. Then, things start to get really bad really fast. In a very short period, credit that once was good is now destroyed.

This means all new credit the consumer applies for will only be approved at high-risk rates. A high-risk rate costs hundreds of dollars more every month and can radically deteriorate the consumer's quality of life for many years.

Most consumers continue to struggle all their life with this cycle. The high interest rates and payments leave them living from paycheck to paycheck. After which, they go late on their payments as they struggle to pay outlandishly high interest rates and payments.

This is the **Bad Credit Cycle**. Many times, it starts with one unavoidable late payment and ends with a lost chance of having a healthy financial future.

Life with Good Credit

Life with good credit is an entirely different story. Many people believe they want to be rich, financially. However, what many do not realize is that the life they dream of has less to do with being rich and more to do with having good credit.

Mercedes Benz is a great example of luxury car that many dream of having. In their dreams, they fantasize about being rich and driving a Mercedes. With good credit, a brand new Mercedes Benz can cost as little as $326 a month. Even a luxury homes can be financed for less than $1,000 a month.

The secret to wealth, in many cases, has less to do with being rich and more to do with credit quality. Even a crazy dream like walking into a store and buying whatever you want or buying a car on your credit is possible if you have good credit even if you are not wealthy.

Good credit will not stand in the way of getting a good job or being approved for new credit at 0% interest rates. Good credit makes living the American dream of owning a home a reality. It even makes driving a Corvette or a Harley Davidson feasible.

Credit lines are issued to consumers based on their credit quality. With good credit, it is common for consumers to receive credit lines and credit cards for $10,000 or higher. In many cases, the interest on those cards is less than 3%, making them useful for many situations, especially emergencies. For this reason, good credit creates peace of mind.

Let me tell you a little lender secret here. Good credit clients, in most businesses, are treated better than those with credit issues are. Auto dealers, banks, mortgage companies treat good credit customers better. Good credit customers get better deals than those with credit issues.

The main reason is that good credit buyers are stereotyped as smart, intellectual, and educated people who do their research and will leave in a minute if they think they are being taken advantage of. Therefore, this fear has most sales managers coddling good credit prospects.

In today's society, good credit is like being rich. When you have it, you are treated better; you can spend more and pay less; and, you can afford to have the life you dream of.

Good credit is the hidden secret of life. This secret to the credit system and the secrets behind your credit scores, plus a proven secret system to correct your credit score will be revealed in the following chapters.

A Consumer's Role in the Credit System

Someone is ensuring that every credit report reflects legitimate and accurate information. This is the common belief I have always heard from clients. They believe that someone, maybe the creditors, the bureaus, or the government is insuring that reported data is accurate and correct.

The sad truth is nobody is monitoring this for the consumers at all. As a consumer, you are the ONLY person involved in your credit who benefits from your credit profile being positive and accurate.

The credit bureaus, like many companies, do have to abide by certain federal and state laws. They are also required to investigate credit disputes based on certain criteria per laws like the Fair Credit Reporting Act. However, the credit bureaus do not question what creditors report, unless they themselves are questioned on it.

Creditors also have to abide by state and federal laws. However, most reporting creditors do not have divisions within their companies where they validate what they are reporting.

The credit bureaus and the creditors do have one thing in common in regards to the reporting of your data. They both make more money the worse your credit is.

Every time you apply for new credit, data is collected. Then, it is submitted to the credit bureau as an inquiry. The inquiry comes back to the creditor as a credit file. Your credit file consists of information on your prior credit accounts, credit score, and residence and employment information. Creditors use this information to help them decide whether to offer or deny you financing.

In most cases, the creditor will not give you a copy of the report they are using. You have to order your own making it harder to ensure the data they are seeing is accurate.

Due to prior credit bureau abuse and misreporting of information, you are entitled to one free copy of your credit report each year. This is because the federal government is not monitoring your report for accuracy. Instead, they are depending on you to monitor your own credit profile.

You have to get a copy of your report each year to make sure it is accurate. When you do this, check all the data very carefully on your report for accuracy. Again, YOU are the ONLY person dealing with your credit who benefits by having an accurate and positive credit.

So, take it upon yourself to get a copy of your free report, dispute any inaccurate information, and manage your credit wisely. You are the only one who benefits when your profile is positive and accurate. Do not forget this.

Personal Credit Score Secrets Revealed

You are probably familiar with your credit score. Nowadays you can gain access to your credit reports and credit scores much easier than in the past because government regulations are now giving consumers more access to this once highly secretive credit system.

Knowing your credit score is important, but knowing how your credit score works is essential. Once you know and understand the components of your credit score, and how they work, you will then be able to make small adjustments and make radical increases to your scores.

The Credit Score Breakdown

There are many credit scorecards in existence today. However, the underlying principal components of all those models remain the same. Some will rate certain aspects of your credit score higher, but the scores themselves are built on the same five ingredients.

Payment History (35%)

Your payment history is the largest component of your credit score. Your pay history accounts for **35%** of your total score. This is based on your prior payment history with your creditors. Late payments, defaulted accounts, bankruptcies, and all other negative information on your credit report have the greatest effect. The more positive accounts you have the higher your credit score will be.

The more recent the late payment is the greater the damage it causes to your credit score. If you go late on your mortgage this month, the Mortgage Industry Option scoring model could drop your scores 120 points or more. That is with only one 30-day late payment!

The said scoring model is based on your potential to go 90 days late on an account within the next two years. Any recent late payment is a big indicator that you will default, and your credit score plummets as a result.

Your creditor cannot report you late unless you are 30 days late, but they will claim they need 10 days to process your payment. So, do not think that they will not report you late because you mailed your payment on the 25th day.

Percentage of High-Credit Used (30%)

If you are carrying high credit card balances in relation to your limits, you can actually hurt your credit score almost as much as by paying the accounts late every month. This is because if you pay late, you affect 35% of your score; and, if you use a high percentage of your available credit, you affect 30% of your score.

This is why I highly recommend to my clients that they apply for new credit. I help them be approved for large credit limit account, such as a $5,000 line-of-credit, that requires no credit check. This high balance account will increase the available credit on their report and increase their score.

This component of your credit score has several different factors. The first factor is the ratio of balances you owe on all of your accounts to the credit limits on those accounts. Your credit score also takes into account the ratio of account balance to credit limit on each of your accounts.

For example, your score will be higher if you owe 30% or less on your credit card accounts. This means, if you have a credit limit of $1,000, you will have a higher score if you maintain a balance of $300 or less.

For revolving accounts, you want to keep the smallest balances while still keeping a balance. Do not pay the account to zero and not use it. If you stop using the account, your credit score will not go higher. Pay it as close to 1% as you can, but make sure you keep your balances below 30%.

Your score will also be lower if it has high balances on installment loans, car loans, mortgages, and other non-revolving accounts. This is why your credit score lowers whenever you open a new account on any of the said accounts. A new car loan, for example, will lower your score once the account is reported. How much lower depends on your spread of other accounts.

As you pay down your loans and mortgages, your score will increase. This is why one of the best things you can do for your credit is open accounts and pay them as agreed. Do not pay those accounts to zero too quickly, as you will not be getting credit for accounts with no balance and no payments due.

The number of your open accounts with balances, the amount of used credit lines, and your account balance on installment loans all of these affect your credit score. You can directly improve your credit score by maintaining lower balances on your accounts or spreading balances over several different accounts. Being approved for new high-limit accounts also increases your score.

Length of Credit History   (15%)

Your "time in the bureau" accounts for 15% of your credit score. The older you are and the longer you have had credit accounts for the higher your score will be. This is why it is near impossible to get a credit score of 800 at a young age.

Being added as an authorized user to an account with a long pay history is another way to increase your score. Keep in mind though that the new scoring models will not give you credit for most authorized user accounts unless you are a family member of the account owner.

If you do have a family member who has positive accounts that have been open for some time, see if they will add you as an authorized user on one of their accounts. You will not be able to use the account unless the owner physically gives you the card though.

Accumulation of New Debt (10%)

This component of your credit score is comprised of how much new debt you are applying for. It takes into consideration how many accounts you currently have open; how long it has been since you opened a new account; and how many requests you have for new credit within a 12-month period.

If you go out today and apply for credit, your creditor will request information from the credit bureaus. This counts as an inquiry on your report. If you have many inquiries in a short period, your scores will be affected.

If you apply for a mortgage today, your scores might drop one point. However, if you apply for a car, a mortgage, and a few credit cards this week, your score could drop significantly. The same applies if you have 12 car dealers pull your credit, or if one dealer has 12 banks pull your credit. Many credit pulls in a short period will have a huge negative impact on your scores.

Do not apply for too many new credit accounts in a short period. Furthermore, do not let many different creditors pull your report while applying for big purchases. Monitor your credit report for inquiries, and dispute any that you are not familiar with or feel should be removed.

Healthy Mix of Credit Accounts (10%)

Your credit score takes into account the mix of credit items you have on your report. This part of your credit score is affected by the kinds of accounts you have and the number of accounts you have for each. Maintain a healthy mix of accounts and this component of your credit score will be golden.

The bureaus will score you higher if you have an open mortgage, three credit cards, one auto loan, and a small number of other open accounts. If you have a ton of credit cards, your score will drop. If you have several mortgages, your score will drop. Any "unhealthy" account mixes will lower your score.

The preferred number of credit cards is three. This means you will actually have a higher credit score if you have three open credit cards than if you have more or less, than three open.

Do not cancel your cards just yet. Remember, 30% of your score is comprised of your balances in relation to your credit limit. So, keep your cards open, but focus on having three large balance cards for better credit score.

Creditors have many models for credit scoring, but the underlying makeup of the score is consistent. Now, you know exactly how your credit score works. With this information, you can make minor adjustments on how you use your credit accounts and see a major increase in your score.

Epilogue

Business credit allows a business to build credit and obtain funding without the business owner being personally liable for the debt. This is one of the biggest benefits and greatest driving factors for any business owner to want to build a strong business credit profile and score.

With a strong business credit profile built, a business can qualify for massive amounts of credit and funding. A business can secure store credit cards, Visa credit cards, MasterCard credit cards, and American Express cards.

A strong business credit profile also helps a business qualify for credit lines, loans, merchant advances, factoring, and many other sources of funding. Having access to large amounts of working capital is essential for a business to grow into a stable and profitable company.

A business becomes more valuable to investors and other parties who might be interested in purchasing the business in the future if it has established a positive business profile, and built a deep and solid credit history.

Business owners can use their established personal credit profiles as leverage for the business to get credit and loans. With business credit established, their business will have double the borrowing power because it will have access to business and personal credits.

Business owners can use their business credit to obtain funding with no personal guarantee. This is a huge additional benefit since the business is not using its owner's personal credit.

Businesses can build good business credit profiles and scores much faster than business owners can build their personal credit profile. Business credit approvals tend to be higher dollar amounts than the amount business owners get through personal credit approvals. Credit limits on business credit accounts tend to be higher. Business credit offers incentives similar to those for consumer credit, such as points and gifts.

Businesses get credit approvals easier and faster with multiple credit sources. It is easier to get approved for multiple credit cards or credit lines with various business credit sources than it is with consumer credit sources.

These are only some of the significant number of benefits that building business credit provides to a business and the business owner. For all these reasons, it is vital for any business to establish a good business credit profile and score, and leverage that to help the business become truly successful.

You are now empowered with the knowledge and tools you need to insure that your business can obtain and maintain an excellent business credit profile and score. Put this knowledge to use today. Get started on building business credit for your business, or use business credit to help you start a new business venture.

Once you have built a positive business credit profile, make sure you use all the tips in this book to grow your business credit and keep your business credit profile good throughout the lifetime of your business. Once you do this, you can finally have the positive business credit and financial future you deserve.

Brian K Howard

Business Credit Expert

www.bkhcreditgroup.com

Resources

http://www.experian.com

www.bkhcreditgroup.com

http://en.wikipedia.org

http://www.sba.gov

http://www.dnb.com/

http://www.equifax.com

www.entrepreneur.com

About the Author

Brian Howard is a noted business credit expert and personal credit consultant. He is the published author of *Credit Made Easy*, a personal guide to understanding your credit.

Currently, he is the Director of Business Credit Services at BKH Credit Group where he specializes in helping business owners establish excellent business credit scores and access cash and credit for their businesses.

Brian Howard is also one of the brains behind the release of one of the top business credit and funding platforms available. His platform is the leading business cash and credit access system in the world today. For more information on business credit scoring, business credit, funding programs, and personal credit restoration please visit **www.bkhcreditgroup.com**

BKH Credit Group

1870 The Exchange Suite 100 #38

Atlanta GA 30339

Made in the USA
San Bernardino, CA
22 September 2016